Jumpstart Your _____, Vol II

12 Inspiring Entrepreneurs Share Stories and Strategies on How to Jumpstart Many Areas of Your Life, Business, Relationships, and Mindset

Compiled by Katrina Sawa
CEO & Founder of JumpstartYourMarketing.com

Get to Know the 12 Inspiring Authors in this Book!

There's ONE page online where you can access all the authors' websites and special offers from this book to make it super easy for you to follow up and connect with them further.

Go to www.JumpstartBookAuthors.com right now before you forget. For a list of authors and their chapters, turn to the Table of Contents page.

Katrina Sawa, Speaker, Best-Selling Author, Award-Winning Business & Marketing Coach to Entrepreneurs Who Want More LOVE in Their Lives and MONEY in Their Businesses!

Copyright © 2019 by Katrina Sawa and K. Sawa Marketing International Inc. All rights reserved. No part of this book or its associated ancillary materials may be reproduced or transmitted in any form or by any means, electronic or mechanical, including photocopying, recording, or by any informational storage or retrieval system without permission from the publisher with the following exception: All authors within this book have the rights to repurpose their own chapters any way they choose to do so.

Published by K. Sawa Marketing International Inc. PO Box 6, Roseville, CA 95661. (916) 872-4000 www.JumpstartYourMarketing.com

DISCLAIMER AND/OR LEGAL NOTICES

While all attempts have been made to verify information provided in this book and its ancillary materials, neither the authors nor publisher assume any responsibility for errors, inaccuracies, or omissions and are not responsible for any financial loss by customer in any manner. Any slights of people or organizations are unintentional. If advice concerning legal, financial, accounting or related matters is needed, the services of a qualified professional should be sought. This book and its associated ancillary materials, including verbal and written training, are not intended for use as a source of legal, financial or accounting advice. You should be aware of the various laws governing business transactions or other business practices in your particular geographical location.

EARNINGS & INCOME DISCLAIMER

With respect to the reliability, accuracy, timeliness, usefulness, adequacy, completeness, and/or suitability of information provided in this book, Katrina Sawa, K. Sawa Marketing International Inc., its partners, associates, affiliates, consultants, and/or presenters make no warranties, guarantees, representations, or claims of any kind. Readers' results will vary. Any and all claims or representations as to income earnings are not to be considered as average earnings. This book and all products and services are for educational and informational purposes only. Check with your accountant, attorney or professional advisor before acting on this or any information. Katrina Sawa and/or K. Sawa Marketing International Inc. is not responsible for the success or failure of your business, personal, health or financial decisions relating to any information presented by Katrina Sawa, K. Sawa Marketing International Inc., or company products/services.

Any examples, stories, reference, or case studies are for illustrative purposes only and should not be interpreted as testimonies and/or examples of what reader and/or consumers can generally expect from the information. Any statements, strategies, concepts, techniques, exercises and ideas in the information, materials and/or seminar training offered are simply opinion or experience, and thus should not be misinterpreted as promises, typical results or guarantees (expressed or implied).

ISBN: **9781674180786**

PRINTED IN THE UNITED STATES OF AMERICA

Dedication

This book is dedicated to Entrepreneurs everywhere who have the desire and mission to make a bigger impact with those they serve.

Here's to creating and enjoying the business and life of your dreams!

Special thank you to my husband Jason and step-daughter Riley who support me 100% on all of my entrepreneurial endeavors. And thank you to all of the awesome jumpstart authors.

*"If you're looking for strategies that can take you from where you are to where you want to be, then **you've gotta work with my friend Katrina**. She's an amazing speaker, author, trainer, coach, and consultant. And I will tell you this: she truly comes from the heart, and she cares about making a positive difference in your life. Work with Katrina today; you'll be so thankful you did."*

- James' Malinchak, Featured on ABC's hit television show Secret Millionaire, Author of the Top Selling book *Millionaire Success Secrets*, and Founder of MillionaireFreeBook.com

Table of Contents

Introduction 1

Jumpstart Your **Abundance**

   Create Greater Ease, Flow, and Love in Your Life

      By Pam Moskwa 4

Jumpstart Your **Balance**

   Keys to Achieving Your Goals Through Balance

      By Shuree Wesley 12

Jumpstart Your **Business**

   4 Keys to Taking Your Business to the Next Level

      By Katrina Sawa 21

Jumpstart Your **Communication**

   Developing Thriving, Healthy Relationships, Even in Conflict

      By Kacie Steinmetz 30

Jumpstart Your **Credit Score**

   5 Steps to Improve Your Credit

      By Pat Walley 39

Jumpstart Your **Health**

   Empowering You to Invest in Yourself

      By Colleen Rekers 47

Jumpstart Your **Joy**

   Create and Live Your List of Joy

      By Jamie Hazen 54

Jumpstart Your **Mindfulness**

   Take Charge of Your Life, One Step at a Time

      By Jason Bittenbender 63

Jumpstart Your **New Reality**

   7 Steps to Change the Way You Think to Get What You Want

      By Sieglinde Van Damme 71

Jumpstart Your **Personal Safety**

   Empowering Yourself to Freedom

      By Cynthia Jolicoeur 81

Jumpstart Your **Profits**

   The #1 Key to More Cash Flow in Your Business

      By Katrina Sawa 89

Jumpstart Your **Relationships**

   The Healing Power of Love and Forgiveness

      By Carolyn K. McGraw 97

Jumpstart Your **Resiliency**

   The Secret to Getting Back Up When You Get Knocked Down

      By R. Mike Garcia 106

Jumpstart Your **Website**

   12 Crucial Must-Haves for Your Website

      By Katrina Sawa 114

What's Next? 122

Introduction

This book, *Jumpstart Your _____, Volume II*, is for you if you need a jumpstart in any areas of your life, career, business, mindset, relationships, beliefs, and more!

I've written a lot of books in my life, a lot of long blog posts and articles, and even recorded a lot of video tutorials and tips. I've also worked with and/or had conversations with tens of thousands of small business owners, entrepreneurs, and people who wanted to start up businesses. One thing I know to be true is that most entrepreneurs and business professionals have a goal of helping people in one way or another.

What I've also found to be true is that all of these professionals, in one way or another, have helped people jump start something. Health coaches help jump start your health, habits, nutrition, and fitness. Relationship coaches help jump start your love life, dating experience, marriage, or a relationship with yourself. And I'm no different: as a business coach, I help you jump start your business, your marketing, your website, your sales, and everything that goes along with running a successful money-making business.

Another thing I know to be true is that most entrepreneurs really do need a book in this day and age. You need to be an author to really be seen as the expert in your industry, or even in the company for which you work. Writing a whole book yourself is a lot of work, takes a lot of time, and sometimes costs a lot of money. Being an author in a compilation book, however, or an anthology book like this one, is a lot less cumbersome, stressful, and costly. It's also helpful when somebody puts it all together for you and you don't have to worry about all the details of editing, cover design, proofing, and publishing.

I've been in business since 2002. I've been an author in seven compilation books, plus two of my own full-length books, and now this eighth compilation book I have put together is the next step in being able to offer my clients the opportunity to become published authors, with very little effort and work on their part. *Jumpstart Your_____, Volume II* is the second in a series of *Jumpstart Your _____* books in which we continue to support new and current authors and they share their stories.

My hope is that, by reading this book, you will learn about how to jump start many areas of your life, your business, your mindset, your relationships, and so much more. The authors that have collaborated on this book with me are experts in their industries and in what they teach. Our goal is to provide a book showing you how and why you will want to consider jump starting many of the areas covered in this book.

If you enjoy any one or more of the stories and chapters within this book, please reach out and contact the author(s). They want to know that their chapter encouraged you, inspired you, or motivated you in some way. They also want to know how they can help you. Each author has provided some kind of next step or free gift at the end of their chapter, to give you the opportunity to learn more. Don't stop with this book: please take the initiative and reach out for more information, more help, and more advice for whatever you might be trying to jump start in your life right now.

Who knows: maybe after your initial read-through of this book, you will pick it up a couple years from now and need to jump start something else. Keep it handy; it might be a life-saver for you sometime in the near future, if not right now. And if you've ever thought about starting, growing, or marketing your own business, and/or becoming an author or speaker, please reach out to me; I'm extremely passionate about helping anybody build a profitable business doing what they love. - Katrina Sawa

Jumpstart Your Abundance

Create Greater Ease, Flow, and Love in Your Life

By Pam Moskwa

Are you ready to create more abundance in your life?

What do you think of when I use the term "abundance"? Do you think of lots and lots of money? Or, do you feel as I do, that abundance is about so many things: time, money, friendship, love, etc.?

It may be surprising to learn that there is a universal law called the Law of Abundance, which states that we are always the recipients of a constant flow of good things into our lives. Most of us, however, do not have lives that reflect this law in action. Even if we may feel abundant in one area, we probably feel a sense of lacking in other areas.

I love to bring awareness about the existence of the Law of Abundance because I don't think that it has gotten nearly the amount of attention that the Law of Attraction (LOA) has.

If I had to choose my favorite universal law between the LOA and the Law of Abundance, I would pick the latter.

The Law of Abundance begs the questions of "How?" and "Why?" How do we "allow" more abundance into our lives? And why the heck aren't we allowing it now? Are we somehow blocking it?

Take a moment to affirm your willingness to allow abundance into your life in all its forms. I know this seems almost too simple to be effective, but your intentions are powerful beyond your wildest imagining.

The Importance of Reaching for a Better Feeling Thought

Too much of the time, we unintentionally use our energy to create things that do not serve us. This happens because the LOA is always at work. Through the LOA, we project our thoughts and feelings, they collect like energy, then they return to us as the people, circumstances, and things in our lives. As with all natural laws, this is a process that works whether we are aware of it or not, like gravity.

We are either creating with intention or creating by default through the thoughts and feelings we think every day. The problem with creating our lives by default is that our lives are usually not anywhere in the vibrational vicinity of abundance.

Think of it like tuning a dial. The energy of abundance is the highest setting on the dial. However, in our day-to-day lives, we tend to idle at a lower setting than the level of abundance. At what emotion is your dial normally set?

Until we become more intentional about the thoughts and feelings we put out into the world, we will continue to be at the mercy of our default thoughts and feelings, and create lives that are in alignment with our emotional setpoint. The key is to become more aware of our feelings, and always reach for the best-feeling thoughts you can in the moment.

At any given point in time, we only have access to those feelings close in vibration to what we are currently feeling. For example, if you are feeling angry, you don't have access to joy because that would be too big of a leap. However, you do have access to blame, which is, surprisingly, higher in vibration than anger. As counterintuitive as it may seem, if you are angry, you will feel a sense of relief when you think thoughts about blaming someone for something - for anything.

Now, although you don't want to linger in feelings of blame, if you can get yourself to that emotional place, you can reach higher thoughts, such as doubt or disappointment. At each new emotional place, reach for a better-feeling thought, and stair-step your way up the emotional scale to the vibrational frequency of abundance.

This is an important process because it helps you stop putting out negative energy and receiving it back in concrete form. You can't control what is happening to you in the moment, but you can always reach for a better feeling thought in response. As you do this, you will find yourself naturally aligning back to the flow of abundance.

To help you stair-step your way to abundance, reach for a better-feeling thought right now. I have a download at the end of the chapter to help you.

Which Reality Do You Choose?

If we find ourselves thinking and feeling the same things we have always felt, we will continue to attract the same experiences as we have always experienced. We may feel as though our lives are stuck, but in truth we are making an unconscious choice again and again.

Our moment-to-moment choices typically don't change our lives immediately, but over time, they shape the direction our lives take. So, I ask you: If you keep thinking the same thoughts and feeling the same feelings, what will your experience of abundance be in 3 months, 6 months, 1 year, 3 years, 6 years, etc.?

For just a moment, close your eyes and imagine yourself in a field of pure possibilities. Think of something you would like to experience. While you are thinking, also allow yourself to feel the feelings you will feel when that event has become a reality in your life.

Your Internal GPS Points to Abundance

The right choices for you are not always obvious. If you must choose between a job that makes you money now, and your life's passion, from which you don't currently see a way to make money, which is the right choice? It can sometimes be difficult to know which choices will align us with a greater flow of abundance.

On the surface, it may seem like choosing the job that brings in money might be the more abundant choice, but is it really in the long term? Fortunately, we each have a unique decision-making strategy to keep us moving towards our highest good, and you can find out exactly what yours is through something called "Human Design", for which I have a helpful resource at the end of the chapter.

Take a moment now and journal about what you've been saying "yes" to that your soul wants to say "no" to, and what you have been saying "no" to that your soul wants to say "yes" to. For each item, visualize how your life might change if you make a different choice.

Let's Talk About Money

One of the biggest ways we desire to experience abundance in our lives is by receiving money, and I have found that we each have a different relationship with money that determines how much money we allow in. If you explore your own relationship with money, you will find that it is a metaphor for other relationships that may need healing in your life, including, possibly, your relationship with yourself.

For example, the way you may feel let down by money is likely the way you have felt let down by other people in your life (and even by yourself). Or, the way you are open to loving money is likely the way you are open to loving others and yourself.

The more you can heal your relationship with money, the more you can become open to allowing abundance to find its way into your life in many forms.

Think about money as though it were a person. Journal about your relationship. Then journal about any connections you see between your relationship with money and your relationship with the important people in your life, including yourself.

All Roads Lead to Love

Everything I have written to this point can surely begin to increase the abundance you allow into your life. However, I would like to share the fastest path to abundance, and it is the simplest, yet likely the most surprising one.

The truth is that love is really all there is. And if love is all there is, that means that everyone is love, including you. And if love is all that exists, it must mean that money is love, also. And if money is love and you are love, then you are money. You and I and money are all made from the same substance. We are all made of love.

So, to experience more abundance in your life, you must spend more time feeling love in all its many forms in your life. Because love = money = you.

Your Next Step:

I created a special webpage for those of you reading this at www.PamMoskwa.com/jumpstart. On that page, you'll find a host of tools and downloads to support you in jumpstarting your abundance, including:

- The Emotional Guidance Scale, to help you stair-step your way to abundance.

- Your Free Guide, "24 Ways to Raise Your Vibes." Abundance is a frequency, and doing things that feel good is the fastest way to get there.

- Plus, you'll find out how your personal "Human Design" Strategy helps you make decisions that will keep you in the vibration of abundance.

ABOUT THE AUTHOR
PAM MOSKWA

Pam Moskwa is a Human Design Expert, Certified Hypnotist, Abundance Coach, and the author of "The Forever Love Attraction Formula," available on Amazon Kindle. She is passionate about supporting powerful female lightworkers to disconnect from struggle and step into the frequency of ease, abundance, and love. In her spare time, Pam LOVES to dance and sing, play board games, and her current guilty pleasure is Love Island: UK.

Jumpstart Your Balance

Keys to Achieving Your Goals Through Balance

By Shuree Wesley

I have found that there are four simple steps to finding balance in all aspects of life and business.

Whether you are a business owner, an employee, or retired, let's face it, we could all use more balance!

I just happen to be a small business owner, so I'm writing this from a small business owner's perspective. However, you can take what I'm sharing here and apply it to your life, even if you aren't a business owner.

Let's face it: in business, you can't afford to be lazy. If you're lazy, your business can come to a screeching halt - and quick!

Do not listen to the voice that tells you, "It can wait until tomorrow." You cannot say "I will get to it", or take care of it tomorrow. This is like saying "I don't need to eat this week". You might as well go work for someone else right now if you are a business owner and this is how your mind works.

In my experience, if you do make positive changes to reflect your best self in your daily life, the outcome will overflow into your business life. You really need to understand that, if you want to be successful, you need to nurture yourself and your business (or career).

The first thing to think about is that you need to have passion: passion for what you're doing, whether it be a career, a job, or whether you're self-employed. Make sure you are doing something that truly lights you up! Make sure you are passionate about it. You will need to be passionate about your life in general, or feelings of depression and burn-out can set in.

The second thing to do is to know your big goals and write them down.

I love to write my daily goals on paper because it inspires me to GET THEM DONE. It always feels good to me to put the check marks on the paper, reflecting my accomplishments.

Have you given thought to the question, "What DO you really want in life?"

"What IS your big vision?"

Knowing the answer can help you to decide which job or business is right for you, and it can enable you to go through your daily activities with purpose. The answer can help you decide whether or not to continue fostering a relationship. Before I met my husband, I really wanted to attract the "right husband for me." I wanted to open a company, and I had such a huge list of things I wanted to attract and accomplish that I created my very first vision board.

A vision board is a place where you post pictures and words (or sayings) and images of the things that you want. Then you look at it every day to get inspiration and keep your big vision at the front of your mind at all times.

I am not exaggerating when I say that I met my husband three weeks after putting images up on my new vision board about meeting my "perfect Mr. Right."

I am not saying it will happen this quickly for you, but I am saying that your mind holds incredible power over what you write down, and what you see, every day.

When I wanted to reach that seven-figure income in my business, my family encouraged me, knowing that I usually achieve whatever I set my mind to. And of course, within a few years, I reached my goals and beyond. I was so obsessed with feeling the accomplishments that I started to long for more...

The problem was that I was now a little obsessed. I was obsessed with working more and making more money. (This is not a bad thing, some might say.)

However, my family was suffering, and so was my health.

Here are some words of wisdom from my son:

"Practice fairness, tolerance, patience, diligence, courtesy, sincerity, and constantly strive to better yourself spiritually, mentally, and physically. Life is about constant growth, and learning who you are as a person, because nobody knows who they are.

So, what was missing?

I started reflecting on what I used to do before I had my company, and then the answer came to me one day. It was very simple. I needed more balance in my life. I had let things get out of control, and I realized that I needed to do something about it.

I realized that, when I was at my peak potential, I had a very special morning ritual that I did every day to keep me on track.

What is *your* morning ritual? Do you know what I mean by that?

Do you practice self-care?

"Take care of your body; it is the only place you have to live." - Jim Rohn

In my experience, the best way to bring balance into life and business is to start your day doing something that will benefit your mind, body, and soul.

Here are four keys to bringing more balance into your life and business through your morning ritual:

1. **Practice some type of faith.** Maybe it is meditation, or a prayer of some kind. There are no rules. It is all about you.

    Spirituality is important to me, because feeling a connection to something is important to humans in general. Feeling connected feeds our inner soul. It could be your connection to nature that helps you feel good. It doesn't matter what your faith is. I would suggest finding some type of connection, even if it is ten to twenty minutes of meditation a day.

2. **Enjoy a workout of some kind**. I don't care what you do, as long as you do it. Discipline is important. If you are serious about what you do, you must have the discipline to take care of yourself. If you do not have your health, then you have nothing. If you do not like to work out, start with a walk of some kind. Walk with a friend. If you have no friends (in many cases,

business owners have very few friends), jump on a treadmill and listen to your favorite music. Just make sure you take care of *you*.

Health and fitness are important aspects of how you will achieve your goals. Feeling good inside will always reflect on your outside. Even choosing the right foods is a must in feeling balanced in your life. I am not saying that you cannot enjoy an occasional slice of pizza. But if you want to feel alive and thrive, then you should choose to eat what will feed your mind and body. Unfortunately, I learned this lesson very early on, after being raised by an obese, unhappy Mother. I soon figured out that her choices in food led to her lack of motivation and many illnesses to follow.

I absolutely love how I feel after a nice run, a walk in the park, an occasional weight-lifting session, or some yoga.

3. **Spend time with your family**. Families are the key to living your best life. Make sure you reach out to someone you love at least once a day by phone, text, or email. Make plans with them. Find time for them. If you lose touch with the ones you love, then you lose touch with the purpose for which you built the business in the first place.

4. **Organize your finances. Your business runs by planning and working on your finances.** I wouldn't still be in business if I didn't tend to my business's finances on a daily or weekly basis. I certainly wouldn't be enjoying seven-figure revenues without paying attention to this aspect of the business. It's unfortunate that most business owners (and non-business owners) don't pay as much attention to their finances as they should.

I find that people either don't know what they are supposed to be looking at, or else they haven't been taught. Perhaps they don't have professional accountants, bookkeepers, or CPAs to supply the correct information.

Deciphering the "numbers" is not something that comes naturally to many, but that doesn't mean it should be avoided. Remember your big goals and vision? How will you realistically achieve those goals without clearly mapping out your finances?

Don't wait until it's too late to make these changes. Don't wait until something happens and you have to take time off work, or your business struggles, or someone you love gets sick. Life is too short not to live in the now. Last I checked, there is no "someday" on the calendar, only Monday, Tuesday, etc. (You get the point.)

About a year before I wrote this chapter, life "happened" to me and my family, and it hit hard.

We were one of the families affected by the CampFire in Northern California during November, 2018. It was one of the deadliest fires on record. We lost our home and almost our daughter and grandson too, plus half of our business. We are still rebuilding as I write this, and it's not easy, but it is important to move forward. We have faith, our family, our health, and our finances. We have a successful, still-thriving business, and we're rebuilding the home and business with renewed strength. We feel that it will be better than it was before.

I'm thankful and grateful for all that I have, and through it all, I am still inspired to write, speak, and transform lives through my stories, wisdom and life-long experiences. If any of this speaks to you, I would love to have a conversation with you and find out if, or how, I can support you with jumpstarting your balance, your life, and even your business! **You can reach me through my website at www.MSWtree.com.**

ABOUT THE AUTHOR
SHUREE WESLEY

Shuree Wesley and her husband Marc are the owners of M&S Wesley Tree Service in Paradise, California. After surviving a horrible tragedy, she and her family were forced to rebuild and stand alongside a dedicated community of friends and, now, fellow survivors. She is an award-winning speaker, investor, author, and coach to other entrepreneurs who know they are built for more, who know they can build a business about which they're passionate, yet aren't sure how. She's studied Real Estate and criminal justice and, because she believes in a strong community, she sits on several boards as well.

Jumpstart Your Business

4 Keys to Taking Your Business to the Next Level

By Katrina Sawa

As a business and marketing coach, I see thousands of small business owners struggling every year, and that breaks my heart.

They struggle to generate consistent cash flow. They struggle to find balance between work and family or personal time. They struggle often with decisions relating to their business, marketing, and growth.

Let's face it, it's not easy being a small business owner. It hasn't been easy for me, that's for sure. We don't know what we don't know, right?

I'm constantly learning, listening, testing, and putting myself out there.

When I first decided to start my business back in 2002, I was working as a Marketing Director at an Assisted Living Facility. I had only been there for 6 months, and I knew it wasn't the right industry for me. Plus, my boss was not someone I could trust or count on, which didn't help.

Before that job, I had sold advertising for the local newspaper, which turned out to be a job I really grew to love. I loved meeting and interacting with the small business owners with whom I came into contact each month. They had real passion, drive, and perseverance. The problem was that they didn't have a lot of marketing and sales training!

I saw businesses going out of business too often. It was so sad. I realized back then that I knew a LOT about marketing and selling, and I could help those business owners with more than just selling them ad space.

When I told my "starter husband" that I wanted to start my own business doing marketing consulting, he *said* he was supportive, but as it turns out, he wasn't really.

As it turns out, he had more of a scarcity mentality, but at this time I didn't know it. I was more of a risk-taker, a true entrepreneur; he was not. Now I refer to these different views as Entrepreneur vs. Employee Mindsets - and they are WAY different. Typically, you find married couples who possess opposite viewpoints, which, without the proper communication, can really harm those relationships.

Well, you guessed it, we ended up getting a divorce. I wasn't willing to go back and get a job after I had gotten a taste of being my own boss, and he wasn't willing to learn more about my true purpose, passions, and goals. Ultimately, it was a really great decision to break up, because having someone who really doesn't believe in you or isn't 100% supportive of you can really harm your entrepreneurial spirit, and you need that positive spirit with you constantly because it takes a lot to maintain your confidence and motivation.

After the divorce, I was free of negativity, but I still had a long road ahead of me to get where I am today.

I had a bout with my own ego in the early days, too. I thought I knew what to do, and I didn't always heed the advice of those ahead of me, or even some of the mentors that I had paid for advice!

Then of course, there is the constant doubt that creeps in and tells you things like: "Who are you to charge that, or do that?" and "You're not good enough," and "Insert YOUR head trash in here."

So how do you combat these thoughts, feelings, and emotions that sabotage your productivity, motivation, and success?

Well, I've learned a few things over the years that helped me, and maybe they'll help you too.

Are you ready to scale your business, or take it to the next level fast?

Whether you're newer in business, or you've been in business for a while now, there is a "next level" toward which you can strive.

I want to share with you the 4 Keys to Taking Your Business to the Next Level, which I've found have been instrumental with my own life and motivation.

1. **Know your Vision** – Understand your BIG VISION: think bigger, expand your mindset to include even greater possibilities. This isn't as easy as you might think. Because we "don't know what we don't know," we often can't SEE what else is possible for us, and we need someone else to look at what we're doing, planning, and thinking in order to make suggestions and give us bigger ideas.

    One thing you can do to keep your big vision "on top of mind" at all times is to create either a vision board or vision video. You can cut out pictures, images, and words that represent what you truly want in your life or career, and paste them into a vision board to keep in your office and look at every day to stay inspired. If you prefer using videos or images with music, you can do the same with a vision video - just don't forget to actually bring it up and watch it every day!

2. **Strategy** – The strategy that has been working for you for the past few years may no longer be working; you may need to shift your strategy and your mindset to try something new, learn a new skill, or hire a team. Often times, this revolves around marketing, lead generation, and sales processes within your business, mainly because of advances in technology and the expansion of what's going on with the Internet. There is NO way any of us can keep up with ALL the new trends while running our businesses, which is why we want to be constantly learning and continuing to hone our skills in these areas.

Keeping a budget for some ongoing learning and mentoring is a must, especially when it comes to learning new and creative marketing and sales strategies. As a general guide, I usually recommend attending one entrepreneurial training every quarter, plus spot-coaching with professionals who can teach you specific things that are on your radar each year. For example, a couple of years ago, I wanted to really enhance my Facebook marketing and connecting, and I attended two separate conferences and trainings specifically focused on that topic.

3. **Support** – It's not just about getting support for your business by hiring team members, staff, employees, and other trusted advisors. You might also need some attention in your personal life. Taking your business to the next level requires YOU to go to the next level as well. That means you must let go of thinking that you "know it all," or you can "do it yourself."

Is it time, perhaps, for you to hire a housekeeper, a landscaper, or a personal chef? Treat yourself, you deserve it! Invest back in YOU and in your business, and you'll live a happier, more fulfilled life as you and your business both continue growing.

4. **Confidence** – Now, if you don't have confidence and you can't figure out how to get it, then running your own business might be a rough road ahead. However, clarity on the previous 3 Keys usually provides more confidence. But the negative (toxic) people in your life can squelch that confidence at the drop of a hat if you don't watch out. Getting help and working on increasing your confidence is a very worthwhile action step. And if you need some support while figuring out this step, there are confidence coaches, life coaches, therapists, and I even do this with my clients! After all, you won't be a very good sales or marketing person in your business without believing in yourself!

As an example of this, about 6 years into my business, I hired a mentor to help me get to the 6-figure mark ($100,000 in revenue). I'd been coasting along (pretty stagnant) at around $70,000/year in my business, some years being a little better and some not so much.

By most people's standards, I was doing very well. But not for mine.

I knew that hitting $100,000 in revenues in my business would change everything for me. Not only would that be more per year than my parents had ever made in their lives, but it would put me in the category of the top 5% of entrepreneurs (which was what my ego wanted). What I didn't realize was that getting to this level of revenues was just the tip of the iceberg, and it was not nearly enough to actually live on for a lifetime.

My mentor pushed me that year, and he pushed me hard. He pushed me so hard, in fact, that I cried a lot during our one-on-one meetings, and in our group mastermind events, too. He had processes and mindset work that was new to me. Before him, all I'd really learned was the practical, tactical stuff you needed to know in order to make money and grow your business.

He never really told me what to "DO" that year to increase my revenues to $100K, but I sure learned how to "BE." And it was the "BEING" that turned me into the successful entrepreneur that I am today. If you aren't sure about what I mean about "BEING", then stay tuned, or watch for my emails, and you'll learn the real keys to running a successful, consistently profitable business!

If things have become stagnant in your business, then it's time for a jumpstart! Many people come to me with this problem. They've been in business for a number of years and they've made a certain amount of money, but then they become **STUCK!** They don't know what to change: is it their business model, marketing, or structure? They don't know what they don't know. They want more, but aren't sure how to get there. They can't see what to implement, add to, or delete from their marketing and strategy in order to take their business to the next level.

If you'd like to have a conversation to review your Big Vision, Strategy, Support System, and Confidence, and see what I can suggest for you to take your business to the next level, then sign up for a complimentary business planning session with me. This session is totally free for those of you reading this chapter, but please don't wait. Life is way too short to wait for success and happiness. **Sign up now at www.JumpstartYourMarketing.com/FreeCallWithKat.**

ABOUT THE AUTHOR
KATRINA SAWA

Katrina Sawa is an award-winning international speaker and business coach known as the JumpStart Your Biz Coach, because she kicks her clients and their businesses into high gear! She is the creator of The JumpStart Your Marketing® System, Jumpstart Your Business in 90 Days System, author of *Love Yourself Successful,* and International best-selling author of *Jumpstart Your New Business Now,* and 4 other books, 10 total to date. She loves to inspire and educate other entrepreneurs on how create a strategy to develop, market, and monetize a consistent money-making business doing what they love.

Jumpstart Your Communication

Developing Thriving, Healthy Relationships, Even in Conflict

By Kacie Steinmetz

It is part of the human experience to occasionally get overwhelmed with emotions or situations.

During overwhelm, in a state of stress, the primitive instincts take over, making the choice for reasonable and rational conversation seem out of reach when we need it the most. I can help you create an environment where you can build and develop healthier relationships, by sharing some tools with you to help reduce or eliminate the need for the primitive brain to run the show (i.e. start an argument). And should there seem to be no way out of a conflict without an argument, using genuine words to stay on track is a win-win for everyone involved.

Consider the following...

"It is 10:45! Why are they still awake? Stop getting them riled up!"

"It's vacation! They're just having a good time!"

"When do WE get to have a good time?"

"What? I thought we WERE having a good time! You're so ungrateful…"

All these words were spoken in a shout-whisper in our beautiful bedroom of the family cottage overlooking the ocean vista: the conflict was in strong opposition to the relaxing venue.

Does this type of "dialogue" and scenario sound all too familiar?

This is the Cliffs Notes version of a "lively intercourse" between me and my husband one summer, a dialogue that was actually about us *wanting to spend more time together.* I threatened to leave two days early, since it *clearly* didn't matter if I was there or not - a suggestion to which he quickly and vehemently responded that I should do just that.

There was so much subtext in our conversation - all I wanted was some of his time and attention, without the kids demanding it at the same time. Why *those* actual words were not used until after we had said some especially nasty and hurtful things to each other, remains a mystery. I am, after all, by trade, a coach who specializes in communication in relationships! How could we possibly have gotten it so wrong?

Crazy things happen in the brain when we find ourselves in heated conflict, or simply not getting what we want or what we think we deserve. We forget the commitment we made as a team, and we get carried away by the importance of protecting the ego. The ultimate goal is to get what we want, but the best-case scenario is when that goal is accomplished in a respectful or even an affectionate way, simultaneously reaffirming our partner's value in our life.

Though my example represents communication in the context of a romantic relationship, genuine and deliberate communication is of the utmost importance in all of our closest relationships: family dynamics, both immediate and extended; dynamics with friends and community; dynamics within the organizational constructs of our professional lives, such as employer/employee or client/vendor relationships. Oftentimes, these are people with whom we relate on a daily basis, and though we haven't chosen extended family and business colleagues in the same way we've chosen our spouses and friends, those relationships are no less important to our health and well-being.

In *The Power of the Other*, Henry Cloud states that meaningful relationships sustain the physical connections hardwired in the brain...it is in relationships that our minds are actually built." It is in our best interest, to ourselves and to the greater good of our communities and our world, to nurture deep and meaningful relationships. Being in conflict doesn't have to be in direct opposition to that end; it actually can help strengthen and develop relationships. It is in the space of community that we learn who we are and develop our best selves.

The most authentic, healthy relationships are most easily created and nurtured between two individuals who are self-aware and ready to grow their awareness together; there has to exist a willingness to explore a deeper connection to oneself, and how it affects the relationship. It is beautiful how Oprah put it: "Our capacity to love and celebrate other people is directly connected to our ability to fully love ourselves." When we understand who we are and the beauty, and sometimes pain, that lies within, we are open to others in a more profound way. With that knowledge, our relationships become pure and powerful. When we understand that everyone has something unique to offer, not only are we able to celebrate ourselves, but we can also appreciate the magnificence of everyone else. It is human nature to do all that we can to protect the ego self, but we must make a conscious effort to allow ourselves to be genuinely known by others who are important to us and, in turn, see them for who they truly are.

Recognizing that other people are mirrors that reflect our beliefs can be an excellent tool for finding patience in a heated conflict. Jen Sincero's example from her book, *You Are a Badass*, portrays this so well. "Would you be offended if someone kept making fun of how short you were if you were 6 feet tall? It most likely would not even register, or if it did, you'd just think they were kind of strange. But if they teased you about being bossy, and deep down you feared you were, it would definitely get your attention." We do not engage in conflict if we don't feel an attachment to that thing of which we feel accused. If you can rest in the truth of yourself, but also recognize that you have blind spots, then you can pause a moment to identify the nerve your offender has triggered. Once the light is reflected on your difficult truth, which was previously subconscious or unknown, having confidence enough in yourself to take ownership and self-correct is preferable to the need for your ego to defend itself. Defending oneself is a direct path to an argument; curiosity regarding trigger points and the speaker's subtext is an excellent way to avoid an argument. Being curious about our reactions to the things that are reflected in other people can then help us to respond in a way that builds connection and cultivates joy.

For example, a work colleague is harshly over-critical of my contribution to a project. I can get curious first about what actual truth lies in the criticism and accept the words that serve me, but I can filter out his anger or frustration, because I am self-aware. I know my purpose, my skill level, and I have confidence in my work. I can then respond to my colleague in a respectful, unemotionally attached way that will help keep the project on track and, as a side effect, by not investing in his emotions, perhaps I can calm his irrational reaction. I could also choose not to take his feedback personally, recognizing that he may be working through some personal or professional struggles of his own.

Of course, a key factor in the aforementioned scenario is knowing that I've given my best contribution to the project (or relationship). If I haven't, more than likely it will be difficult, if not impossible, not to take my colleague's (or loved one's) reaction personally. Our best selves vary in different environments and situations, but knowing ourselves and our capabilities enables us to give our best to each endeavor at the appropriate level. Doing so allows for confidence and space to be curious and accept the useful truth, not the garbage thrown our way in someone else's moment of carelessness. Their words may seem hurtful, but read between the lines and find how the subtext is helpful.

On the flip side, if we recognize that we did not give our best, then the shortest path to diffuse any situation is to take ownership of our shortcoming and - you guessed it - sincerely apologize.

Relationships are complex, but it's important to note that where we invest the most, we get the best return. Once we understand the core beliefs and habits we bring to the table when we engage in relationships, it is more possible to be curious about ourselves and those with whom we choose to engage in a heated debate. That curiosity can help us identify our own true needs and then choose words that mean what we really want to say with respect and affection; this can quickly extinguish the spark in a discussion that is beginning to heat up.

Humans thrive through connection. No matter your past or the pain you carry, that healthy connection is possible. The strong foundation of our families and our society depends on it!

What's Next?

I have created a special page on my website with a few tools and opportunities for you. **Please visit www.KacieSteinmetz.com/jumpstart for access to these exclusive benefits:**

- **Cheat sheet** with tips for how to maintain healthy communication in conflict.

- You can **join my online yoga and mindfulness community** to get grounded and become more self-aware so your relationships can be more pure, deep, and rich.

- **Video series** for new couples who want to ask the important foundational questions. (Find out more about that launch on my website.)

- Discounts on programs, events and trainings.

- I always welcome the opportunity to connect directly; **let's schedule a complimentary discovery call during which I can help you** create an environment for deeper, purer connection with the ones who really matter.

Be well, friends, and make your day fabulous.

ABOUT THE AUTHOR
KACIE STEINMETZ

Kacie Steinmetz is a Relationship Coach and Natural Wellness Champion with her Life Coach Certification from Coach Training Alliance. She helps people who are in complicated or difficult personal and professional relationships learn to communicate authentically and with purpose. She's also a Richway Amethyst BioMat addict and distributor, a Reiki practitioner and Yoga instructor. Kacie believes that feeling well in body and confident in spirit leads to more genuine connection, respectful communication, and, subsequently, more joy in relationships.

Jumpstart Your Credit Score

5 Steps to Improve Your Credit

By Pat Walley

It was 1970, and I was facing the biggest challenge of my young life. You see, I was 4 years old and had just caught myself on fire, literally. The resulting 2nd and 3rd degree burns covered most of my right leg. Looking back now, this was a pivotal moment for me and shaped my future in so many ways.

My mom saved my life by putting out the flames before I was consumed. It's funny how we remember things from our past. I remember lighting the corner of my pajama pants with the lighter and I remember running down the hall, terrified and on fire. I don't really remember the pain that night (the pain that came later - I will never forget), but I do remember that it seemed to take forever to get to the hospital. I can only imagine how scared my Mom was as she watched me fade in and out of consciousness, wondering if I had just died in her arms.

I had sustained 2nd and 3rd degree burns over most of my right leg. It took hours of surgery, a huge skin graft, and nearly 300 stitches to patch me up. My leg was burned so badly, there was little hope of normal growth or being able to bend and flex.

I spent the next 2 months in the hospital. My typical day consisted of lying in bed, watching other people in wheelchairs and on crutches, hopping around. My right leg was a bundle of bandages and I could not move it. I figured I was probably going to be disabled for the rest of my life. How would I ever play soccer or ride a bike or run with my sister? So many of the things I enjoyed, like climbing trees, would be forfeited. I really just wanted to be normal again. But how could I? My leg was destroyed. I struggled with this reality day and night, for weeks. I distinctly remember one morning, as I watched one of the adults wheeling himself across the ward, my life changed forever. I decided I was NOT going to be crippled. Period.

I believe God honored my choice and began a miracle in my life. From that point on, the idea of hobbling around was no longer an option. I envisioned myself playing in the yard, climbing trees, playing football, running, and everything else all the other kids got to do. When I experienced the suffering that accompanied healing, I pushed through it. My goal was clear. WALK.

After nearly two years of therapy, and countless failed attempts, I finally took my first tentative steps. Hooray! I beat the 90 percent! I knew I would be running soon.

So, what does this have to do with Jump Starting your Credit Score? Let me explain:

In my story, I set myself on fire. Ignorance and carelessness stopped my normal life in its tracks and created a ripple effect for years to come. Everyone around me was impacted. I couldn't do the things I wanted to do. Every day, I dealt with the fallout of burning my leg. Recovery seemed hopeless at times. I did eventually recover, but only after a decision and massive effort.

Fast forward to my adult life. My own credit story was difficult. I was in debt from divorce and poor choices, and my credit score was below 500. Early in 2009, I drew a line in the sand and vowed that I was not going to be crippled by debt and bad credit. I still remember when I got approved for a $500 card and began to Jump Start My Credit Score. My results are not guaranteed to be your results. Using one of the tips below, I was able to increase my FICO® score by almost 50 points in one month. I was then able to get qualified for 0% credit and began my credit recovery.

My mission became clear: empower others to improve their credit profiles and increase their scores so they could get out from under the crushing interest rates and become debt free. So, I started my company, Dignity Credit Solutions. We are blessed to help give people hope when their financial future seems hopeless. The problem is that, just like I didn't understand how quickly a lighter could destroy my leg, so many of our clients don't understand the extent and speed that careless financial habits can cripple them. When I meet people who have dug themselves into a deep, deep hole, I recall how dejected I was when I had my own credit issues, and I feel their pain. Debt and high interest rates are stopping many from living a better life. Recovery seems hopeless and, sadly, some people take their own lives to escape the oppressive weight of massive Credit Card Debt. The good news is that there is hope. Issues like maxed-out credit cards, bankruptcies, and collections are difficult, but can be overcome. Success in this endeavor takes a decision, action, time, consistent effort, and help.

Our training and tools empower people to raise their credit scores and qualify for lower interest rates. Then, the money that was going to interest payments is available to pay toward the principle and accelerate debt paydown. What may have taken years to pay off by making minimum payments can be reduced to a few months. This works for most types of debt.

Here are my 5 steps to Jumpstart your personal credit score and begin your own journey of hope:

1. **Decide to change today.** Then implement a plan to get out of debt. There are many resources, including Dignity Credit Solutions. One of the most crucial steps is to make a budget and stick to it.

2. **Pay ALL your bills on time.** Payment history makes up **35%** of your score. This has the biggest impact and is entirely in your control. If you already have late payments, don't be late any more. ***SECRET** The timing of when you pay your bill can actually improve your score.* Find out when your credit cards report to the credit bureaus (Experian, Equifax, TransUnion) and make sure your balances are at the lowest on that date. This can have dramatic results. **Example:** If one of your cards reports on the 19th, you could pay your bill on the 15th or 16th then do not charge anything until the 20th. When the balance reports, it will be at its lowest. (I used this strategy to increase my FICO® score nearly 50 points in one month.)

3. **Get all your revolving credit (credit card) balances below 30% of the available credit limit.** If the card has a $1000 limit, find a way to get the balance at $299 or lower. 10% balance is even better. The amount of your available credit that you use makes up **30%** of your score. This tip can improve your credit score DRAMATICALLY.

4. **Stop applying for new credit.** Each inquiry can drop a score 10 points, even if you're approved. New accounts make up **10%** of your score. The length of credit (how long you've had your accounts) makes up **15%** of your score, so don't close old accounts.

5. **Have different types of credit accounts, such as mortgage, car payment, credit card, and loan. 10%** of your score is determined by how you manage different types of credit.

If you are fortunate enough to have little or no debt, and enough cash-flow so you don't need credit, then you are in a small minority of Americans. Credit scores and profiles are checked when purchasing a home, a car, even a phone. Poor credit can disqualify hard working adults from these purchases, and low scores cost consumers millions of dollars in interest payments. Shockingly, nearly 90% of consumer credit reports contain errors that drag credit scores down. Poor credit and low scores can be transformed into high scores and good credit.

The question is universal for those struggling with obtaining and maintaining a good credit profile and score:

"How can I do that?"

Visit our website www.DignityCreditSolutions.com/jumpstart for the resources you will need to answer that ever-present question and schedule an appointment for a free credit profile review and strategy session.

How did I do it?

I still bear the scars of that fateful encounter with a lighter.

There was pain and struggle as I grew and healed. Eventually, I was able to play football, run, ride bicycles, hike, dance, and bounce my children on that same knee that was reconstructed in 1970. God was by my side when I faced overwhelming odds with my leg - and my credit. I believe that, since I was willing to do the work, He was willing to do the rest and perform the miracles.

Unlike a burn, credit wounds heal much faster, and the scars eventually disappear. If you are willing to decide to change and commit to doing the work, you, too, can regain your dignity and break free of the shackles.

ABOUT THE AUTHOR
PAT WALLEY

Pat Walley is passionate about helping others succeed. For over 25 years, he has worked with 350+ businesses in 48 states, training owners and employees in point-of-sale systems, basic accounting, and successful business practices. His specialty is simplifying complex things. Pat is also a gifted speaker and writer. Audiences immediately connect with his stories and have fun while learning. He founded Dignity Credit Solutions to equip consumers and businesses with the tools to win. Most consumer credit reports have errors and nearly 90 percent of businesses fail. Pat's mission is to help them overcome the 90 percent.

Jumpstart Your Health

Empowering You to Invest in Yourself

By Colleen Rekers

Luckily for you, I'm NOT going to talk about deprivation, drinking celery juice, popping diet pills, downing disgusting protein shakes, or running to the bathroom with a colon cleanse in this chapter. I've been there, done that.

As someone that has struggled with her weight her entire life, I've tried so many fad diets that I've truly lost count. Each time I chose a different health route, I believed I had found the "thing" that was going to change my life. However, with each attempt came failure again and again.

I was that girl, the girl who felt unworthy, insecure in her body, highly self-conscious, and who even avoided pictures. I put on a good front and I really tried to consciously ignore the fact I wasn't happy, but inside, I felt so broken.

I had every excuse in the book, and I honestly believed I

just had bad genes. I would sit and watch the beautiful skinny girls eat slice after slice of pizza and I felt as though I was getting heavier just watching them take in those calories. I felt hopeless.

After law school, I married a man who loved me just the way I was. I may not have truly loved myself, but it was reassuring knowing that someone considered me beautiful on the inside and out. After a struggle with infertility, we were blessed with twins. Unfortunately, I spent most of their childhood avoiding taking pictures with them, as I didn't want to ruin the pictures by being in them. I look back now at where I was, and it saddens me that I let my lack of self-worth stop me from documenting the love that I had for my precious children as they conquered each and every milestone.

Two years later, in an attempt to have another child, we ended up pregnant with triplets. I think I was in shock at first, then overjoyed, then terrified as I came to realize what a high-risk pregnancy I had ahead of me. The pregnancy took its toll on my body, and I was hospitalized several times. My husband lost his job, and we were drowning financially with two-year-old twins at home. I gave birth to triplet boys in an emergency C-section at 25 weeks. It all seems like a blur; my three babies were born in critical condition.

Thankfully, with prayers from family and friends around the world, I healed and my boys and I were eventually able to come home. Not long after returning to work, I became a single mom to five young children, as my soon-to-be ex-husband chose a life of addiction. It was a devastating time, and my life became all about survival. Self-care: what was that? I was focused on giving all I had to my children. Even with a single income, I wanted my children to have everything, and to never ever feel like they had to go without. I can look back now and say I'm proud of the mom I was for them; my children are amazing, but I also acknowledge it was a very hard time for me. My mental and physical health was extremely poor; I was exhausted, and I wasn't one to ask for help.

I started to have some health issues, and it terrified me. I was a single mom who was also an only child, whose father had passed, and whose mother didn't live in town. And I didn't like relying on anyone else. The only thing I could think about was what would happen to my children if I was hospitalized for health issues. The fear over who would take care of my children weighed heavily on me. It was at this moment I made one change, one small change, that snowballed into where I am today: 150lbs lighter, and healthier than I have ever been.

I did it "the hard way," as I call it… I made little changes to what I put in my body, and I dove into personal development. Some of the pounds were coming off, but it wasn't easy. I was a little "all over the place," still had a negative mindset, and I hadn't found a game plan that I could incorporate into a long-term lifestyle. At this point, I decided to join a gym, and for two years I worked out 5-6 days a week consistently. I finally realized that it wasn't just about working out, as you can't "outwork" a bad diet. It was really all about two things: mindset, and nutrition. Get your mind and your nutrition right, and get results, even without exercise, which was contrary to what I had always believed. Clients tell me all the time that when they initially decided to lose weight, the first thing they did was join a gym. Don't get me wrong, I absolutely love to exercise and my gym is the best, but if you truly want results, it's about mindset and nutrition.

I get a lot of accolades from people who have seen my weight loss journey or who have come to know what I've accomplished. I really couldn't be prouder of myself, but honestly getting the weight off isn't what excites me most; it's how I feel. I really thought all the health issues, aches and pains, lack of energy, etc., were all normal – part of aging. I was so wrong! And I didn't realize how important my mindset is.

I had watched a girlfriend of mine transform her life before my eyes, and I wanted to know more. My initial response was negative. I was highly skeptical, thinking "Here I go again, chasing the 'thing' that will change my life." To my surprise, it was actually the "thing"! After two weeks, I knew that this was different, and my analytical, legally trained brain started doing all the research to understand why it was different this time.

Nutrition, supplements, vitamin-enriched products, and/or exercise aren't cures for diseases or ailments. Our bodies, by design, are built to fight off disease, sickness, etc. If you fuel your body properly, then your body is able to do its job, a job that it's naturally really good at. I have seen people even with stage four cancer say that our products aren't a cure, but the quality of life this nutrition gives them is life changing. Unfortunately, for a number of reasons, we are not always able to get everything our bodies need from what is offered at the local grocery store. The fact is that most of us need more!

My finding is that if you pour optimal nutrition into your body, your body's response will be to run at its optimal level. For some, that is weight loss; for some, it is weight gain or muscle gain. And did you know that optimal nutrition can also be a game changer for both adult and youth mental health? The most important thing to realize is that your health is an investment, not an expense, and if you jumpstart your health, all areas of your life will prosper.

I now fill my body with vitamins, nutrients, and superior nutrition. I don't measure, I don't count calories, I don't eat fake food or pre-made insta food. I eat real food. I don't have a "can't have" list, I don't feel deprived. I feel satisfied and full of energy, now that my body is being properly fueled and running at its optimal level.

I do things differently than most. As a life and health coach, I work with you to discover what is holding you back from living your life to its full potential. I want to get to know you and why you are sabotaging your success across different areas of your life. I know first-hand that there has to be a mind shift coupled with optimal nutrition so that your brain and body can start working collaboratively to propel you toward what I have to come to know as "true health". After years of experience, research, and trial and error, I have also chosen to partner with a billion-dollar health and wellness company, Isagenix, that can complement what I am able to offer my clients.

Today, I am beyond blessed to say that I'm in a loving relationship with an amazing man, and together, we have seven beautiful children. I don't consider my health and wellness journey over, as its ongoing, but I am now healthier both mentally and physically than I've ever been. I'm blessed to offer personalized coaching to others so they, too, can take back their life at any age, and under any circumstances. Let's do this together!

Grab my free Guide, 5 Quick-Start Steps to Jumpstart Your Health, online at www.JumpstartYourHealthWithColleen.com!

ABOUT THE AUTHOR
COLLEEN REKERS

Colleen Rekers is a life and wellness coach, speaker, writer, and entrepreneur, who also runs a successful Isagenix business. Her training, education, research, and life experience have catapulted her into life coaching, wellness, and personal development areas. With her unshakable belief in, and dedication to her clients, their success is inevitable. Colleen Rekers resides in Northern California with her family of nine, and passionately serves clients all around the world.

Jumpstart Your Joy
Create and Live Your List of Joy

By Jamie Hazen

What is **Joy**?

How many books have you read in your search for Joy or Happiness? I have ready plenty, and I have a stack of favorites in my bookshelf. I've found that I can't find joy in a book. Instead, I have to act in my own life to create my Joy. What about you?

Merriam-Webster defines Joy as:

1) a: the emotion evoked by well-being, success, or good fortune, or by the prospect of possessing what one desires; b: the expression or exhibition of such emotion,

2) a state of happiness or felicity

3) a source or cause of delight

A synonym for Joy is Happiness.

I personally define Joy as an inner peace I feel. You know that feeling you get when you are in a moment, reflecting on something or someone, and smile? I'm not an expert in this subject, nor on your life; I am, however, on a constant journey to find Joy (and balance) in my own life.

Who am I and how do I find Joy?

I got married and had my two sons at an early age. I thought this was a great idea because I knew so much better than my parents. After that I married the first time for 20 years; I was then divorced for almost 10 years. I then married my soul-mate and was blessed with bonus gifts: one step-daughter and two dogs. Both of my sons and my step-daughter have grown up to be outstanding humans whom I love dearly, and who make me proud. I also had the good fortune to spend 20 years at a job that I loved in city government. This career allowed me to retire at the age of 50 with a pension and medical benefits so I could start my own business and do work that I love, plus volunteer in my community. In addition, my mother moved back to California, near me; all of these things bring me great Joy.

One thing I've learned is that, the more books and chapters I read on finding my Joy, the more it keeps my quest at the forefront and reminds me of my goal. I love reading books and listening to podcasts about other people's goals and journeys toward joy and happiness. An excellent read is anything by Gretchin Rubin, author of *The Happiness Project* and *Better Than Before*. I also like, *I've Been Thinking,* by Maria Shriver. I also love to listen, read and watch anything by Mel Robbins – she makes me feel like she is speaking directly to me, like she wants me to succeed at everything I do; I refer to her as my virtual BFF.

How do you find Joy?

How should you start your quest for Joy? If you've read any of those types of books I reference on my bookshelf, you probably know to write down the top 10 or 20 people or activities that bring you Joy. Have you done this already? Where is that list? Did you file it in a binder or planner somewhere that was retired at the end of the year? I personally have many of those lists. So, I ask you to take some time now to create your List of Joy as a work of art for you to reflect on daily. This could be the last time you create this list, or it could be perpetual, whatever you choose. Make it *yours* and *amazing*.

Or as an alternative to a LIST, you can create a visual for yourself in a vision board - a vision board of what brings you joy, so that you can look at it daily to remind you to make time for some of those things.

A constant reminder equals constant action.

What are some things that can go on your Joy List or Vision Board of Joy?

Ask yourself:

- Who do you love hanging around?

- Where do you love being? (In nature? Watching movies? The gym?)

- Do you have hobbies? What do you love doing? (Or what do you wish you spent more time doing?)

- Are you a foodie, and do you want to experience new foods and restaurants? Make more dates with friends to do that.

- Are you someone who wants to travel more? If so, where?

Here are a few things that bring me Joy – hopefully this will help you get your list started:

- Time with family and friends (this girl loves a good BBQ, Happy Hour or Taco Night)

- Listening to music (Live music at concerts are a fave)

- Reading (mostly motivational or self-encouragement books – this ignites a fire in me to be my best self)

- Creating in my planner (can you say stickers and sparkly gel pens? I love colors!)

- Early morning walks (when all is quiet and it's just me and my own thoughts)

- Sitting on the beach just listening to the sound of waves (the beach is my happy place)

- Wine tasting (red wine is good for the heart, I'm told)

- Sewing (although I don't dedicate enough time to this now, I remember how joyful it used to make me when I finished a fun project)

- Dancing (another activity I need to invest more time in – I can't even line dance, yet)

- Volunteering (Children, Empowerment and Active Duty/Veteran Organizations are my passion; what are yours?)

- Tacos (tacos by themselves bring me joy, but they are even better when eaten with friends or family, with guacamole on top)

- All things Starfish (the starfish is my spirit animal – they are beautiful and can be very colorful)

- Socializing/Networking (this girl loves a good party, chit-chatting and getting to know people)

- Thrift store shopping (and finding that perfect "item" at a great price - perhaps it's starfish related)

- Reflecting (looking through scrapbooks and reviewing pictures on Facebook – I love the feeling I get when I review my month in my planner before flipping to the next month, and also looking at pictures that bring back fond memories)

- I'm even learning to find Joy while doing some public announcing, i.e. I'm the emcee for a few local concert events (although sometimes it's also a bit scary)

- And, as it turns out, I found great Joy in writing this chapter for the book.

If anything on my list matches yours, feel free to copy; I'm happy to share my Joy. Make your list. Color it with your flair. Frame it. Hang it as art in your special place.

I recently asked a friend what Joy meant to her. She responded that a joyful life for her was the success of her friends and family. It's also a life without undue chaos.

Will every day in your life be Joyful? Unfortunately, the answer is no. The keyword here is "life," and inevitably, there will be ups and downs.

Have you ever lost a family member or friend? Have you ever had your heart broken or been divorced? I answered yes to both of those questions. How do you overcome the not-so-joyful times in your life?

My first experience with grief was when my "boyfriend" died when I was 12 years old. That was a very sad time in my life, and I was too young to know how to process those emotions. I hid it from my parents, but I cried myself to sleep every night for a long time. I even wrote a poem about him and his tragic death; I can still recite that poem today, 40 years later. Counseling would have been a great plan for me to manage my grief, but hardly anyone went to counseling back then. If you are dealing with tragedy or grief, I encourage you to talk with someone who can help you get back on your road to Joy.

Does your career bring you joy, or do you work in a job that just pays your bills? If it's the latter, what are you doing on your "off work time" that sparks Joy for you? If you've got this, good for you. If not, act immediately – there are so many opportunities and organizations out there waiting just for you.

Motivational speaker Jim Rohn said: "You are the average of the five people you spend the most time with." Are these people joyful? If not, it might be time to mix things up and choose new people for your inner circle. You don't have to dump your old friends, just make some new ones and spend quality time getting to know them and mimicking their best character traits.

My favorite poem is titled *Live Your Dash,* by Linda Ellis. It's about the life you live from birth to death. I encourage you to look it up and read it, and Live Your Dash - Joyfully.

In closing, my goal for those reading this chapter is to keep your quest for Joy in the front of your mind; as I stated earlier, a constant reminder equals constant action. Don't forget to create, and live your List of Joy. **I'd love to connect with you and support you on your quest for more Joy! You can connect with me online at www.JamieHazen.com/jumpstart.**

ABOUT THE AUTHOR
JAMIE HAZEN

Jamie Hazen started a consulting business after retiring from a 20-year career with local government. Her background is in administration, project and event management.

Jamie's volunteer work includes the Board of Directors for the Roseville Police Activities League, Performing Arts of Roseville, Downtown Roseville Merchants, Downtown Roseville Partnership, and the Placer County Visitors Bureau. She is also on the team that brings the annual event PlannerCon to San Francisco, CA. Jamie is also a proud Blue Star Mom with a son working in Army Intelligence.

Jumpstart Your Mindfulness

Take Charge of Your Life, One Step at a Time

By Jason Bittenbender

Mindfulness is the cognitive process of paying attention to the world around you in the present moment. But in today's fast-paced world of instant information and gratification and constantly looking for the next big thing, we tend to lose sight of the beauty of life around us and how we play a role in it.

When I was a kid back in high school and college, I was full of life. I always saw the beauty around me and actively sought out beautiful places to explore. In fact, my degree from college was in Parks and Natural Resources Management, and I dreamed of going to go work at Yosemite National Park forever and being happy out in nature. What I found out by working in Yellowstone National Park and Mt. Lassen National Park is that I would be a seasonal worker for about ten years before I could get a full-time position as a ranger in the parks system. There was also no telling where I would end up working (there's one hell of a long line for Yosemite!).

So, I didn't end up going that route for my career. Instead, I entered the corporate world where I worked for Hyatt Hotels, then Enterprise Rent-A-Car, where I met my first (starter) wife, and finally I landed a job as a mortgage loan consultant, a career that I held on to for 13 years - quite the opposite of that initial dream. During my 11-year relationship to a woman with whom I thought I would spend the rest of my life, is when I discovered the true meaning of mindfulness.

It was during that time in my life when I realized that many people were not mindful about those around them (insert my ex-wife here). I would always see the good, and she would always focus on the negative. I was always happy, positive, and extremely helpful around our home. I did EVERYTHING from yard work to cooking all of the meals, taking care of our baby when she was born, all of the laundry, and basically running the entire household while simultaneously serving as breadwinner and working full-time as a mortgage lender. She was selfish, negative, and controlling. I would always take other people into consideration, as I felt in my heart was the proper way to be, and she would be selfish and only do things if she felt there was something in it for her.

Eventually, enough was enough. I finally got out of that situation and was on my own for a while, sharing 50% custody of my young daughter Riley. I was determined to raise Riley to be respectful and considerate of others, confident in herself, and to always see the beauty of life around her. It was over the last six or seven years post-divorce, however, when I really became aware of how mindfulness can play a part in our day-to-day activities.

To me, mindfulness is something that is rarely practiced by most people these days. You never know what people might be going through in their personal lives when you see them out and about, and it's always good to give them the benefit of the doubt, even if they happen to be angry or cut you off in traffic, which are two things I see every single day unfortunately. How we react to the world around us shapes not only the way others view us, but also our own happiness and our view of the world. It is so easy to run around in the rat race and be selfish and impatient. What takes real skill is being thoughtful and considerate of others and the world we live in. The trick is to be mindful of our impact and how it can spread.

I'm now married to my new wife, who has her own business as a speaker, author, and business coach. She has been a huge encouragement to me over the past seven years to stop doing the careers that do not make me happy, such as Mortgage, and most recently, pest inspections. I am finally to a stage in my life where I feel comfortable embracing my own passions. She's the one who encouraged me to start my current business as a voice-over artist. If it weren't for her, I would probably still be doing mortgage, not knowing what else was possible for me.

Venturing out into my own business was something that just came about recently for me, and it was a little scary and exciting at the same time. But now that I'm 50 years old, I have realized that I need to do what makes me happy, not just what brings in a steady paycheck. What's funny is that my new career will probably bring in more money than either of the two jobs I've had over the last 15 years, which I would have never thought possible years ago.

Being mindful of my own needs, desires, and happiness is now at the top of my to-do list. So many of us, including my former self, don't put ourselves first. And let me tell you, that is no way to live. I was diagnosed with tonsil cancer when I was 45. I went through the most difficult and overwhelming time of my life. I endured 5 separate surgeries (one of which had me in the hospital on Father's Day). I agreed to the surgeries in hopes that I could avoid chemo and radiation. Unfortunately, since the cancer had spread to my lymph nodes and glands, I would still have to go through both chemo and radiation. I was stage 4.

Halfway through treatment, the pain from the radiation sores in my mouth and throat made eating solid foods far too painful. I lost 38 pounds on a purely liquid diet and was a shell of my former self. To top it all off, on the last day of radiation, I was wheeled from the cancer center to the emergency room with multiple pulmonary emboli in both lungs. If I hadn't been at the hospital, I would not have made it. It was an experience I wouldn't wish on my worst enemy.

Having my amazing wife, who was my girlfriend at the time, plus a huge outpouring of love and support from friends and family, and a little faith that it would all work out in the end... it did. I am now in full remission from cancer. I have a few skin cancer scares here and there, but that's due to my "fun in the sun" times out in nature.

These days, I am more mindful than ever of those around me, and pretty much still put the needs of my daughter, my two German Shepherd dogs, and my wife in front of my own, but I'm a work in progress. My hope is that I can develop a routine with this new business soon, fit in some personal workouts (which I love), spend more time in nature to feed my joy and decrease my stress level. I plan to live my life full-out, enjoying all it has to bring.

The beautiful result in all of this is that my own happiness and awareness of my impact on the world have made it easier for me to be mindful of others and spread happiness, encouragement, and kindness. These spread from within, and can be very contagious. It takes a little effort, but it is well worth it.

My goal for you is that you will be mindful of your needs, desires, and your own happiness from this day forward. Life is too short to work at a job that you hate, suffer in a relationship that is not serving you, or live a life without joy and true love. When you are able to free yourself from what does not serve you, it becomes much easier to share in your happiness and success. Try practicing the following on a daily basis:

- Take 5-10 minutes each morning to meditate and clear your mind of negative thoughts and self-talk.

- Be considerate of those around you.

- Have more patience.

- Be generous with encouragement and compliments.

- Acknowledge the good in people.

- Be aware of your impact on the earth and the people around you.

- Don't take things personally; it's more than likely not about you anyway.

The more we all do this, the better a place the world will be for all of us and our children.

For more information about me, follow me on Facebook, under Jason Bittenbender. **For more information about my Voice Over Talent work, reach out to me at www.JLBVoiceOverTalent.com.** I'd love to serve you in any way I can!

ABOUT THE AUTHOR
JASON BITTENBENDER

Jason Bittenbender grew up in Oakland, California with his mother, father and older sister. He attended college at CSU, Chico where he spent much of his spare time riding his mountain bike in the foothills near town. He is a father, husband, and full-time voice-over artist living in Roseville, CA. He has worked a variety of jobs which have given him a multitude of experiences working with people. He is passionate about helping others and experiencing the beauty of nature.

Jumpstart Your New Reality

7 Steps to Change the Way You Think to Get What You Want

By Sieglinde Van Damme

Are you alarmed that life is flying by too fast? Would you like an easy process to reset your goals and make clear decisions so you feel alive, energized, and in control again?

Unlike wishful daydreaming, let me introduce you to a 7-step creative process to think outside the box while keeping one foot in reality so that your new life—your new reality —is easily achievable, affordable, and sustainable.

You see, when I immigrated from Europe to the US, I had to adapt to a new society. I had to re-imagine not who I was, but who I "could be" on this side of the ocean. This was such a gift because it made me realize we all have more choices than we think.

I learned that a choice is an opportunity, and I embraced my opportunities with both hands.

I went from being an insecure newlywed with a conservative MS Economics degree, to an internationally exhibiting and award-winning artist. And after obtaining a second Masters Degree (in art), I went from a restrictive 9-to-5 schedule to fully unleashing my creative and intellectual potential as a successful entrepreneur.

To this day, I still explore the idea of "what else is possible" as a dynamic of defining and redefining visual realities in my artwork. As a strategic communications consultant, I use this concept to get surprising results for my clients. Then one of them said:

> **"Sieglinde, what I like best about working with you is that you can think outside of the box while keeping one foot in reality so that whatever strategic plan or grand idea you come up with, it's actually feasible."**

That's when I realized I had unconsciously developed a very keen thought process to explore and reach goals, while facilitating easy change. And now I share this 7-step thought process with you, so you can also benefit from this approach.

Step 1: Pause and Go In

Stop forcing, pushing, doing, reacting and making things happen on the outside. The first step is to take a moment and cut out the noise.

Don't worry, there is plenty of opportunity to allow reality back in, including other people's opinions, comments, unsolicited advice, and your own excuses for why something can't be done. You can pick those back up later on if you insist. But for now, please close the door on the outside world and GO IN.

If you already have a practice in place to clear, quiet, and open your mind, congratulations! Whether it is meditation, yoga, journaling, or some other practice, keep doing what you're doing if it works for you.

If not, I have an exercise for you at the end of this chapter, to flip your mind temporarily away from the analytical, I-need-to-figure-everything-out-in-my-life.

Step 2: Explore the Core

Now that we have pointed our minds in the right direction, let's explore.

If you are eager to jumpstart your new reality, that means something is not sitting well with how things are right now.

So, what do you REALLY want?

Or, start with what you absolutely do not want.

Whatever starting point you choose is fine; however, the ultimate goal still is to discover what it is you DO want.

Once you have your starting point, let's use seven layers of "why" to help you uncover what issue is really at the core of your dissatisfaction.

Example:

1. I don't want to work at my current job anymore.

   Why?

2. Because it drains me.

   Why does your job drain you?

3. Because I am not motivated to do the work.

   Why are you no longer motivated to do this work?

4. Because I never wanted this job to begin with but the money was good so I took it. But now the money is not motivating me anymore.

   Why is the money not motivating you anymore?

5. Because I don't have the time or the energy to actually enjoy my money! Feeling drained also keeps me from spending quality time with my family. I don't feel connected with them anymore.

   Why do you feel disconnected from your family?

6. I feel I am just the money-making machine and I want my presence to matter to them.

Why do you need to be reassured your presence matters to them?

7. Because I love them and I don't want to lose them.

In this real-life example, the job itself is not the actual problem. The real issue is an insecurity about the safety, love, and appreciation of family. You can still change jobs if you want, but now you know that a closer connection with your family is your real priority.

Knowing the underlying reason "why" you want something to change helps redirect your next move toward the direction of where you really want or need to be.

Step 3: Keep an Open Mind and Be Surprised

Before you can think outside of the box, you need to explore the boundaries of the box first, including the good, obvious, silly, stupid, dumb AND bad ideas. And when you completely run out of ideas, that's precisely when the creative part of your brain gets activated and the juicy stuff comes out.

Rest assured that we'll get to the editing part later, but for now, let's enjoy a judgement-free brain dump. Be curious and come from a place of possibility rather than fear, lack, desperation, or limitation. This step is meant to be FUN!

Core Process:

Take a stack of Post-Its and work in columns. Post your main goals at the top (such as more freedom, more love, more money), and add any ideas that might get you there on a different color Post-It underneath.

Keep going until you run out of ideas completely, and then go some more. Remember, the most creative part of your brain gets activated when you think you have no more ideas left. Do some extra research if you have to.

When you are confident that all potential options (good and bad) have been acknowledged, re-organize your Post-Its.

Are some ideas related? Group them together.

Connect ideas across columns that you would never have imagined to be connected before. Allow yourself to be surprised!

Now, pick 3-5 ideas you are really drawn to and explore them even further.

Step 4: Embrace the Chaos

At this point you might start to feel uneasy and overwhelmed. Multiple options are staring you in the face, but choices have consequences. Relax and take a really deep breath.

No one is asking you to decide just yet. Simply accept that chaos is an inherent part of the process and the only way out of it is through it.

I like to compare it to a kitchen remodel. At some point, your old kitchen will have to be demolished, and for a while you'll have no kitchen at all - only dust and debris. You don't know what the new kitchen will be like, but you do know for sure that the kitchen will never be what it was before. The only way to move is forward, and that's a good thing, because you would never have remodeled your kitchen if you were happy with it to begin with.

While chaos is an inherent part of change, some chaos can be avoided. Therefore, do take step 5 to heart.

Step 5: Slow and Deliberate

Fear, self-doubt, and lack of commitment are the biggest roadblocks to successfully implementing change. However, familiarizing yourself in advance with your future life will ease some (or all) of these barriers.

Our brain is always on a mission to keep us safe and, as such, prefers familiarity above all else. Instead of fighting an uphill internal battle, give yourself the space and time to familiarize yourself with what lies ahead, and your brain will become less resistant to change.

Act, feel, and believe as if your new path(s) are already unfolding. This is also the right time to refine the vision of your new reality and alter or edit ideas before going full-out.

Moving slowly and deliberately will boost your self-confidence and build confidence that you are doing the right thing. No more self-sabotage: you've got this!

Step 6: Commit

Action! This is where a lot of people come to a screeching halt. And sadly, their goal remains a dream, a "someday" project, and nothing more.

You now have two choices.

You can decide that playing it safe is the smarter way to go. If this is your choice, I respect your decision. However, what keeps you safe today inevitably becomes your (self-imposed) prison tomorrow.

The other option is to stick with the steps you have taken so far, and take them to the next level.

But where to start?

Don't use overwhelm as an excuse for the easy way out. Instead, become the ultimate project manager of your new reality. With a clear focus on the end goal, reverse engineer to determine what needs to happen first. Break down the overall goal into bite-sized steps so that each individual action feels comfortable and manageable.

Step 7: Evaluate and Celebrate

Take time to evaluate and celebrate - not just your end result, but the little wins along the way as well.

Because if you did it once, you know for a fact that you can do it again!

What's Next?

The above is a simplified version of a carefully crafted creative thought process that can be tailored to facilitate change in your personal and professional life, and to solve complex business problems.

Each step also corresponds to an art/mark-making equivalent, giving you the option to try on this new way of thinking in a safe environment. After all, there are no mistakes in art!

Sign up for free access to a very powerful breakthrough-to-clarity exercise at www.Sieglinde VanDamme.com/jumpstart. You can also contact us online with questions or for information on upcoming workshops and programs to experience this process in-depth (individual or group setting).

ABOUT THE AUTHOR

SIEGLINDE VAN DAMME

Sieglinde Van Damme is an award-winning artist, creative entrepreneur, and business communications strategist. As a holistic left-brain/right-brain thinker, she achieves superior results by consistently infusing analytical reasoning with creative thinking skills, while grounding creative concepts into realistic possibilities. The 7-step process to Jumpstart your New Reality is a model formula of her signature process.

Sieglinde holds an MS in Economics degree from the Catholic University of Leuven (Belgium) and an MFA in Photography. She taught at SJSU and worked with startups and entrepreneurs across Silicon Valley. Her artwork and writings have been exhibited and published across the globe.

Jumpstart Your Personal Safety

Empowering Yourself to Freedom

By Cynthia Jolicoeur

Have you ever felt vulnerable going out by yourself or being home alone? Have you ever been worried about what might happen when you're out on a date or at a march or a rally? Have you ever been concerned about a person or situation at work?

Many people (especially women) don't know what to do if they find themselves in an unsafe situation, and so they either avoid thinking about it or worry that they'll just freeze and do nothing.

Many feel frustrated with even having to think about safety while going about their daily lives, and yet the "but I shouldn't have to" mindset can lead them into more danger.

If you're ready to stop feeling vulnerable, apprehensive, and unprepared, what can you do? Do you have to invest several years and lots of money in training to master a martial art? Should you buy a firearm or other self-defense tool, and hope that having it will keep you safe? Is hiring a personal bodyguard the solution?

The reality is that jumpstarting your personal safety is much simpler and quicker than any of those options.

The first step is to change how you think about self-defense.

The person responsible for your well-being is you. If you're involved in an incident where you have to act to protect yourself and your loved ones, you can't outsource your safety to anyone else. Depending on where you live, help in the form of law enforcement, security staff etc. can be anywhere from several minutes to an hour away. You can't guarantee that a spouse/significant other/courageous bystander will always be on hand, or that they'll be ready and willing to intervene in your moment of need.

The only person you know will be there is you. When danger threatens, you must be your own first responder. The good news is that whether you know it or not, you are already well-equipped to protect yourself!

Many people think that self-defense is all about fighting. The truth is that, unless you are ambushed, most potentially dangerous situations and interactions can be recognized and avoided or de-escalated before violence happens.

The importance of avoidance

The most important ability you have is your ability to detect possible danger. Your brain and body are wired to be an early warning system. Unfortunately, humans are the only creatures who actively dismiss those warning signs! So, if you want to stay safe, you must listen to your instincts and intuition, heed any "bad feeling" that arises, and understand that there is no downside to acting when a situation or person feels "off".

One way to avoid danger is to set strong, clear boundaries. A boundary could be "Back off! Don't come any closer!" or "Stop commenting on my appearance."

If you set a boundary and it is ignored, restate it and let the other person know what the consequence of crossing the boundary will be. For example, "If you come closer you will not like what happens to you," or "If you keep making personal comments about me, I will report you to Human Resources."

If your boundary is crossed, you must apply the consequence! Many people, especially women who don't want to be thought rude, state a boundary and then do nothing when it is crossed. That will set you up to be taken advantage of, and possibly harmed. Setting a boundary is not the start of a negotiation!

If you can't avoid danger, you may be able to protect yourself by defusing, de-escalating or changing the dynamics of the situation. Remember that you don't have to act like yourself in a situation that seems like it may turn ugly – you can play whatever role you need to, and say whatever you need to, with the goal of extricating yourself from the situation without harm.

Preparation is the key:

Take a moment to think about your personal reason to survive an incident. There's something in your life right now that you are passionate about, that can help motivate you to act when you must. For many years, my personal reason was my elderly mother, who lived with me and relied on me to advocate for her and support her as she went through the closing years of her life. I knew that if something happened to me, she would be left with no help, love, or support to see her through her final days. Think about your reason, and revise it as your life changes.

Consider what it could cost you if you encounter danger or violence and don't act. Many people immediately think, "Well, I could die." And that's true. But that's not the worst case. You could disappear and leave your loved ones wondering what happened to you, for the rest of their lives. You could end up paralyzed or comatose, hospitalized for decades, becoming a financial burden to your family. You might never be able to see your children grow up, marry, have their own children, etc.

Give yourself permission to act. Many people worry about appearing foolish, paranoid, racist, or offensive. Criminals count on that concern to keep you frozen and unresisting.

Learn how to navigate through fear. Fear does not have to immobilize you, and you can learn how to break free of its grip. In fact, fear can be a wonderful catalyst to energize you and help you act. If something happens, don't get stuck in thoughts of "This can't be happening, oh no, this is crazy," and don't let mistaken beliefs (like "If I get shot I will die," or "There's no way I can do something when my attacker is so much bigger than me") limit your ability to act.

Get to know the "bad guys":

Learn to recognize and avoid predatory behavior. You may not be able to identify a potential attacker by how he or she looks, but you can learn to identify common ways in which attackers try to manipulate potential victims and how they set up the process that will get them what they want. They may use threats and intimidation, or try to establish rapport and develop a personal connection. They may interact with you over the course of weeks or months, or your encounter may only last a few seconds or minutes. That all depends on what they want.

I highly recommend reading Gavin DeBecker's book *The Gift of Fear,* in which he describes what he calls

"Survival Signals" – the most common manipulations used by asocial predators bent on abduction, rape, and murder.

Know how to fight if you can't avoid or defuse a situation.

The good news is that you don't have to train for decades or earn a Black Belt in order to do that.

If you need to respond to danger physically, all you need to do is tap into the natural abilities with which you were born. Your body is designed to protect itself. It comes with reflexes that will protect you before you can even think about what to do, and tools that you can use, including your elbows, knees, nails, fingers, teeth, and others.

Your goal is to use your tools on whatever targets are close and accessible on the person who is attacking you, and to keep going until that person can't continue to try to hurt you.

Many people worry that they won't be able to successfully fight off an attacker, because they assume that the attacker will be bigger and stronger. Even the biggest, strongest, meanest predator in the world will focus more on his pain than on you if you crush his trachea or drive your thumb through his eye. What matters is your willingness to do whatever it takes to be safe.

Along with your natural weapons, you may be able to use a defensive tool you carry with you (such as pepper spray, a firearm, or a disguised weapon like a tactical pen), or an improvised weapon (something nearby in your environment that you can turn into a weapon).

If you're fighting for your life and what you are doing isn't working, most likely you are not using enough force.

There is a lot more to learn and know about how to protect yourself; I've only just scratched the surface here. Please just don't hide your head in the sand and get at least a little more educated about this because you never know what can happen. I would invite you to visit my website or have a call with me for more information. I want to help you be more prepared.

Your personal safety lies in your hands.

You cannot control whether or not a criminal or predator decides to target you, but you can control how prepared you are and how you respond to any potentially threatening situation.

Are you ready to unleash your personal power and create some *Freedom* in your life?

Go to www.CynthiaJolicoeur.com/jumpstart to book a Personal Safety Consultation, download your free copy of my guide, "10 Must-Know Ways to Avoid Being Assaulted," and watch the free webinar, "Best-Kept Secrets of Personal Safety."

ABOUT THE AUTHOR
CYNTHIA JOLICOEUR

Cynthia is a 4th-degree black belt, self-protection expert, and host of the Born to Be a Badass podcast, a unique and groundbreaking show about women, violence, and safety. She teaches women how to be safe in any situation by learning how to deal with danger, to navigate through fear, and by discovering their inborn strengths, power, and skills. Listen to the Born to Be a Badass podcast for a weekly episode focused on violence, safety, and building a great life.

Jumpstart Your Profits

The #1 Key to More Cash Flow in Your Business

By Katrina Sawa

In my Business and Marketing Coaching and Education company, I am constantly redefining myself, my services, and my products in order to stay ahead of, or at least keep up with, the industry of marketing. If I don't bring fresh ideas and material to my clients regularly, then someone else will.

Most entrepreneurs, however, are not taking enough time to work "on" their businesses, therefore they tend to struggle and stress out. Oftentimes they comment, "I'm too busy," but their busy-ness isn't productive.

As a small business owner, you have to wear many hats, but your Sales and Marketing hat is the single most important hat you wear. How much time are you spending wearing that hat?

Here are 3 action steps you can take to work ON your business so you can be more productive and make more money:

1. **Schedule one day each month as a "Creative" Day** – a day in which you will do nothing but sit and write down all the ideas that come to mind about how you can update or increase your business. These include people with whom you can collaborate, how you will promote the products and services you offer, what else you want to add to your website, and what is the next "big thing" you want to create or launch. This is important because entrepreneurs usually have a TON of ideas, but no time to implement them all. This day will give you the extra time to discern which ideas are more viable than others and even perhaps develop a plan for them.

2. **Schedule another day each month as an "Implementation" Day** – a day you will do nothing but put ideas into action. This could include updating the copy on your website, writing and distributing press releases or email promotions, planning a workshop, developing marketing materials, reaching out to joint venture partners, calling, and organizing. If you don't stop to implement, your ideas won't become a reality or they won't get done very well. It takes time.

3. **Schedule weekly time to work "ON" your business** – typically I recommend a minimum of 2-10 hours each week to spend on marketing,

sales, follow-up calls, email marketing, strategizing, and delegating. This time is in addition to your in-person networking and your customer appointments. If you're not very busy now, then spend more like 60% of your work week on these revenue-generating tasks. Even when you DO get a full client load, you still want to allot 2-5 hours a week on marketing and sales, but perhaps it will be more in a capacity of nurturing, educating, and upselling at that point.

Then, beyond actually plotting out the time to spend ON your business, you need to know WHAT to do to become more profitable.

Here are 7 easy Revenue-Generating tasks on which to spend your time:

1. Calling through your database – pick up the phone if you want to make money!

2. Record a quick video tip and upload to YouTube and other social sites.

3. Write a quick blog post and share it with your social sites or subscribers.

4. Request to speak for 3 potential organizations, conferences, meetings, or radio shows.

5. Get to one, two, or even three networking events in person every week.

6. Create your own free or paid teleclass, webinar, or event for list building or sales.

7. Send an email out to your list asking for referrals, or making an offer on something they can buy.

And here is what really determines whether you will become more profitable or not:

The #1 key to more consistent cash flow is to SIMPLIFY what you're doing or selling.

A couple of years ago, I was trying to grow my business, and a mentor told me to create this new product and this new program and this new service. After a year or so of doing all that and pretty much launching something new every other month, what do you think happened?

You'd think I would have made oodles and oodles more money, but sadly, that did not happen. The revenue came in small chunks and, because I had so many different ways to buy or different ways to learn (i.e. products, programs, services), my customers and prospects were confused. They never knew which thing to sign up for, so attendance in many of these new programs was not as high as I'd hoped.

Then what do you suppose happened? Yep, I got tired. I was tired of working so hard to sell *The Next Big Thing*. I was tired of constantly trying to reinvent a new thing that I thought people would want to buy.

When times were tough and the market was down, it seemed like this was the right thing to do: keep trying to find the thing that people would buy. But it wasn't.

The best thing I could have done was to simplify what I had to offer.

I'm extremely clear about what I'm offering these days, how to buy it or sign up for it, *and* I don't have to kill myself in the process. You see, what matters most to your prospects and customers is not that you have huge amounts of things to offer them, but that you have the "right" thing that they "need and want."

Here are a few tips on how to simplify your business:

1. **First off, figure out what your ideal clients and customers really want**. Learn what matters most to them about what you offer rather than what *you* think they need or that they should buy. They will only invest in what they see they need and want, not necessarily in what you think they need.

2. **Next, determine all the different ways you could offer those things to them**. Could you develop a live workshop or virtual group training rather than deliver the information one-on-one? Could you design or develop a product, program, or something that they could buy without any personal involvement from you after the purchase

is completed? Figure out how your ideal client or customer wants the information, training, or how they need your product delivered, and make sure you offer it to them in their preferred manner - not necessarily the way in which you want to deliver it. I talk to prospects a lot about their learning styles and suggest products and services that I offer based on how they want to learn or digest the information. Most of my prospects actually prefer one-on-one attention, for example; they are not as good with programs for which they have to be self-disciplined.

3. **Choose price points that are realistically in the range of which your ideal clients and customers would typically invest.** You can stretch beyond that if you choose, so you have room to negotiate or offer "special deals." Just make sure you also take a look at your overall product/program mix so that you do have some lower-level offerings as well as some higher-level offerings. If you desire to make a certain amount in revenue this year, then you want to make sure you have enough opportunity to sell enough products and services. Crunch the numbers for what you're selling multiplied by how many you think you can sell, to make sure you can hit your goals. (Ask me about the *Easy Yes Offer* training that I share with my one-on-one clients and event attendees!)

4. Finally, you won't make anywhere near the amount of sales that you want if you don't do enough marketing. Marketing is a huge term; it encompasses so many things, and not all marketing strategies are good for all types of business owners. So, you do have to be careful which ones you implement. You want to give each strategy a fair trial period before you decide it doesn't work, but first you need to start out with a very smart, effective, and consistent marketing plan. Your marketing could be simplified as well. There are so many ways to automate, systematize, and delegate your lead generation, marketing, and follow-up tasks; this is something to really focus on if you want better results. You'll need to do a LOT more marketing than you think in order to become hugely profitable!

It's not too late to simplify your business! You WILL gain almost-instant focus and revenue. If you need help in simplifying your business products, services, or marketing, then let's schedule a complimentary strategy session and get some CLARITY! Sign up for a one-on-one private strategy session online today at www.AskKat.biz. You can also find more trainings, audios, programs, and products on the Products Page of my website, or on the Free Trainings page at www.JumpstartYourMarketing.com/freetrainings.

ABOUT THE AUTHOR
KATRINA SAWA

Katrina Sawa is an award-winning international speaker and business coach known as the JumpStart Your Biz Coach, because she kicks her clients and their businesses into high gear! She is the creator of The JumpStart Your Marketing® System, Jumpstart Your Business in 90 Days System, author of *Love Yourself Successful,* and International best-selling author of *Jumpstart Your New Business Now,* and 4 other books, 10 total to date. She loves to inspire and educate other entrepreneurs on how create a strategy to develop, market, and monetize a consistent money-making business doing what they love.

Jumpstart Your Relationships

The Healing Power of Love and Forgiveness

By Carolyn K. McGraw

There is no love without forgiveness, and there is no forgiveness without love. - Bryant H. McGill

Just imagine how it would feel to enjoy happier, more fulfilling relationships. You have the power to transform, repair, and upgrade your relationships right now. Are you willing to let go of the past hurts and love yourself enough to truly forgive?

The most annoying thing in life is...other people! Right? The biggest jerk in your life is really your greatest teacher! Maybe you married or gave birth to this person who was divinely sent to push your buttons, so that you could grow and learn about what you are really made of. Inside your most challenging relationships are hidden gifts with priceless lessons on unconditional love and forgiveness.

Lucky for me, I married and gave birth to my wonderful teachers! My joy turned to sadness the day I gave birth to my first-born son. Before I even took my bundle of joy out of the car and into our home, I remember feeling a dark cloud of sadness hover over me with the thought that I would not have my child for very long.

Later, I learned it was a premonition, sent to prepare me for what was to come. Thirteen years later, my baby was gone...swept up in the ugly storm of a very angry divorce. My precious boy had taken on the same rage as his father, which resulted in my being completely cut out of his life for 12 years.

I tried everything humanly possible to repair our broken relationship. My son began to refer to me as "the mom," hanging up on me each time I called. Before the divorce, Taylor once made me a plate of "I'm sorry cookies," which was his adorable peace gesture after an argument. I later sent him, "I'm sorry cookies," and even took a pizza to his school just to get a glimpse of him. He reacted like I was the worst person on the planet. His best friend, sitting there, looked at me with sympathetic eyes and apologized to me for Taylor's awful rudeness. Years and tears went by, filled with hundreds of unanswered prayers. I chose peace, let go, and went on. I remarried, had another child, and still Taylor was not in my life.

The love lessons I learned from my son:

- Whatever the problem, it is a test in love.
- Stop blaming and judging.
- Love is accepting what is.
- Love the situation now.
- The healing part of love is forgiveness.

Heart Healing

I gathered up my love lessons and took them into my job teaching high school English. It felt wonderful to my heart to share a bit of motherly love to kids who were starving for it. "Write a love letter to yourself" was the assignment. Khayree, recently out of prison, astutely wrote, "You can't really love someone else until you love yourself first."

My students struggled to learn as their anxiety and anger flared up in the classroom. I reminded them that **it's not about what's wrong with you, it's about what happened to you.** I just wanted to heal their broken hearts. Inspiration arrived, and I created Poetry-Therapy, which began with the question, "What do you want to heal in your heart?"

Khayree wrote a 7-page poem about his journey from rage to forgiveness. Another student wrote a tribute poem to his still-born son. After sharing it with everyone, he said that writing poetry was more helpful than counseling. A homeless student told me that one night she felt suicidal, so she decided to write a poem to cheer herself up and was amazed at how much better she felt. Writing and sharing poetry was powerfully transforming and healing. We performed at the State Capital and on TV, getting standing ovations.

The new love lesson my poets taught me is that there is beauty in your pain.

My love miracle finally happened! One day while I was sitting at my desk, my phone rang and I heard a man's voice say, "Hi, this is Taylor." For the first time in 12 years, I heard my son's voice again!

Relationship Mirror

Our relationships are a mirror to our inner world, reflecting how we feel about ourselves and what we believe to be true. The things that bother us most in others are really the things we don't like about ourselves that we've hidden and refused to accept. Be brave, take a real look, and ask yourself what you need to let go. When you can accept your own flaws, the things that bother you in others will fade away.

Love You First

Buddha said, "You yourself as much as anyone one else in the entire universe deserve your love and affection." The relationship you have with yourself determines everything else in your life, such as choices, attitude, and behavior. If you want to improve a relationship, the first step is to accept and love yourself unconditionally. Stop beating yourself up and give yourself a compliment. You deserve it!

Forgiveness is Love

If you want more peace and love, you must learn to forgive. Forgiveness is the highest form of love; it is the healing part. Forgiveness can create miracles in your life and in your body.

Holding resentment creates blockages that limit your progress and your love flow. Decide now to forgive everyone in advance! Bless your relationships with unconditional love and forgiveness.

Set Firm Boundaries

You have the power to set boundaries and not accept anything hurtful into your mind or body. You have the power to refuse poor treatment by others right now! If something is uncomfortable you have the right to say "NO," no matter who it is. You don't deserve to be treated badly, no matter what!

You must believe that you are worth more. Demand respect. Reject negative words by boldly declaring, I don't accept that! Bullies lash out because of their own pain. They spew their crap onto anyone who will take it. You don't have to accept their crap!

If you don't like your relationship, you have three choices: you can either change it, accept it, or end it. You have the power to rewrite the script of how you want to be treated. Stand up for yourself, proclaim your boundaries, and don't accept less. **You have the power to be happy!**

Better Communication

It is vital to communicate your feelings honestly to others. When you don't, it adversely affects your well-being, and can lead to emotional issues. Always speak your truth because you deserve to be heard! You can learn to express yourself without drama in a positive, calm manner to someone who has irritated or upset you.

Here's a quick example of how you can communicate your needs with someone:

Without emotion, say, "When you did this____I felt this____. Next time could you please____?" (Make your request.)

Express your appreciation to others more often. When your kids or partner are doing something positive, reinforce their behavior with a compliment like, "I just love how you do the dishes every night."

Power of Love

Love is a powerful healing force! Love conquers, love opens doors. Love is felt when we are fully present with another. It is a true gift to really look into another's eyes and listen. Children will do whatever it takes to get attention because it equals love to them. Loving words and loving thoughts generate an electric force that literally can be felt by another person subconsciously. With intention and visualization, you can send heart blessings to others that can help them.

Here is a Heart Streaming Exercise that you can do:

Take a few deep breaths and repeat, "I open myself to love…I'm willing to love and be loved."

Now visualize you and your family enveloped in a circle of light and love. Visualize a stream of light and love from your heart to their hearts. Breathe deeply. Who would you like to forgive? Send love and light to their heart and say, "I love you, I am sorry, please forgive me, thank you." Repeat these three times. (Hopono, Hawaiian forgiveness prayer.)

Miraculous Shifts

Forgiving the past hurts can create miraculous shifts in your life! One client improved her finances, family relationships, and love life by forgiving her mother. Within two weeks of the emotional stress release session, she had strengthened the bond with her daughter, landed a top-paying client, and got engaged! She had previously turned down her boyfriend's proposal. Forgiving her mother brought inner peace that opened her up to saying yes to more love!

Love is the answer to all problems!

Are you ready to maximize your brilliance, recharge your health, your relationships and your business? Go grab a free relaxing and empowering guided mediation that I made for you on my website here www.CarolynKMcGraw.com/jumpstart. While you're there, you can also schedule a free Success Strategy Session, and let me help you with your healing, clarity, confidence, and purpose so you can enjoy more loving relationships.

ABOUT THE AUTHOR

CAROLYN K. McGRAW

Carolyn K. McGraw brings peace to the chaos as a Transformational Empowerment Coach and Hypnotherapist. She is also a Speaker, Poet, Author, and Teen Life Coach. As a former TV Host, Carolyn produced her own show called "Life on Purpose" on the Women's Broadcast Network Channel. With a Master's Degree in Education, she taught school for over 20 years. Carolyn has been featured on many TV and radio shows with her inspirational story of transforming the lives of youth from gangs and jail with her Healing Hearts Method using poetry-therapy. Carolyn empowers entrepreneurs to share their messages by transforming their wound stories into wow stories in her program called "Heal it! Write it! Speak it!"

Jumpstart Your Resiliency

The Secret to Getting Back Up When You Get Knocked Down

By R. Mike Garcia

After a serene day spent in Colorado's majestic mountains touring Aurora's water infrastructure, I prepared for a restful night. It wasn't often I got away from my day-to-day duties as Fire Chief. I would soon be reminded that a Chief is never off duty...

The loud ring of my cell phone startled me awake. Instantly, I knew it was not good. But never could I have been prepared for what became the most significant event in my professional life and our city's history.

On the other end of the line was my Operation Chief, who stated that there was an active shooter (or shooters) attacking the patrons at the Century 16 Theater. He was enroute and would update me upon his arrival; there were possibly hundreds of affected civilians.

I turned on the television and the TV reports made it sound even worse! Accurate information in real time was almost impossible to obtain. I felt helpless being so far away, but I knew the men and women of the Aurora Fire Rescue had leadership and training that was second to none. This proved to be true, and their heroic response alongside police, dispatchers, ambulance personnel, and bystanders who stepped up triumphed over evil that night. Over 70 innocent people were wounded and 13 lost their lives.

After the theater attack, it was discovered that the shooter had booby-trapped his apartment with high explosives to act as a diversion in order to kill as many innocent people as possible that night. For many lucky reasons, the explosive devices were never triggered, but the hazard remained for fire rescue and the bomb squad to mitigate.

By that time, I had returned to the city and met with my Ops Chief. He gave me an accurate account of what took place and the ongoing incident at the shooter's booby-trapped apartment. I responded to the apartment and became part of a Unified Command Post to mitigate the threat of explosives. The firefighters at the scene of the theater shooting were the same firefighters now at the booby-trapped apartment; they were responding to back-to-back high stress incidents.

As shift change approached, I was informed of a mental health debriefing that city management had arranged for all responding parties, including fire crews. I was informed, however, that no fire personnel attended the debriefing. This was of great concern to me, knowing the gravity of what had just taken place. Although Firefighters are very seasoned to traumatic events due to the frequent tragedies they face on a daily basis, they too need to get support. Many of the firefighters believed this would be their last call, nonetheless, and they immediately engaged, unselfishly and without hesitation. Their mindset was to save as many lives as possible before theirs were taken. Thank God they didn't have to pay the ultimate sacrifice.

15:13 Greater love has no one than this: to lay down one's life for one's friends.

Upon arriving at the Unified Command Post, a firefighter engineer came up to me and said, "Chief, you need to take this phone call." I looked him in the eyes and could clearly see this was a call I needed to take. On the line was a retired New York Firefighter. He said he was a survivor of the 9-11 terrorist attack, and along with other 9-11 survivors, they had formed a NYFD Peer Support Team that consisted of psychologists, psychiatrists, and other professional trauma experts to help the firefighters deal with traumatic events. They were offering their support, and their Peer Support Team was already in flight on a private plane! This was the answer to my prayers; I knew our firefighters would respond well. They talked to every firefighter who had responded to this tragedy.

How does one recover from such a horrific event as this?

America believes firefighters are invincible, and perform unbelievable rescues without any consequences. Firefighters believe we are stronger, and don't want to show any signs of weakness in front of our peers or the public. "Just doing our job," we say, and "Let's move on to the next call." The truth is, we're human, and need to recognize when we need help - otherwise, Post Traumatic Stress steps in, or worse. I have experience firsthand that one person can make a difference - especially a person who is willing to share their traumatic experiences and is expertly trained to do so. One such person (or team) can make a real difference in another's mental wellbeing. Even the strong need help and God bless the NYFD Peer Support Team. Aurora Fire has since formed their own Peer Support Team that models NYFD. Paying it forward helps the healing process and builds resiliency.

> *"Let the world define Aurora, Colorado not by one man's cowardly and evil actions, but by our courageous response and the millions of prayers, support, and acts of kindness for the victims and their families." - R. Mike Garcia, Fire Chief*

It's been over 7 years since that night in 2012, and of course there is a lot more to the story. I have since retired with 38 years of service, including 9 years as Aurora's fire chief. Those years in service have taught me the true meaning of Resiliency, and many other core values that I live by and teach to my kids. I want to narrow it down to four common factors so you can start learning to be more resilient in your own life. I also plan to speak, inspire, and write a lot more about this topic with firefighters all over the world; this is my new purpose.

1) **Purpose:** I see genuine happiness in others who have a true purpose in life. Simply stated: you have a "why" to get up in the morning. I am blessed that I seemed to always have a true purpose in my life. While achieving my goal of being the first in my family to graduate college, my purpose was becoming a future career firefighter and doing my best to serve my community. I had a strong Mission Statement, Vision and clear values: Professionalism, Respect, Integrity, and Customer Service.

2) **Passion:** One needs passion in his or her life to be truly happy: something to stir the blood. The upcoming football season, skiing, music, running, traveling...I think you get the idea. Once again, my passion was the job, but my true passion has always been my family. I loved

being a firefighter and being a part of something greater than myself. I developed into a team member who could be trusted, promoted up the ranks, and practiced servitude leadership.

3) **Camaraderie:** We are not meant to be alone. Those who have family, significant others, friends, club memberships, and affiliations are walking around with smiles. They share their lives, good and bad, with others. They have someone to pick them up when things are bad and someone with whom to share their good times. They learn from others and share their knowledge. I know of men and women whose best friend is their dog! In the fire service, camaraderie is second to none. Our friendships are forged under fire and life-threatening incidents. We trust one another with our lives, and at the drop of a call we are there for one another, no excuses, no hesitation.

4) **Looking Forward:** Having something to look forward to is essential to being happy. Living for today may sound good, but having something to look forward to is the spice of life. It could be something as simple as the changing of the seasons, a vacation, or training for and running a marathon. Once again, my job always had me looking forward to the next challenging call. I also looked forward to getting back with my fire company to hear how they spent their time off of work. Most firefighters are very adventurous,

and I couldn't wait for the stories that they men brought back to the firehouse.

Your Purpose, Passion, Camaraderie, and Looking Forward, however, are worthless if you don't have GRATITUDE! At some point, we will all have bad days, hit a wall, or feel betrayed. What gets us through these difficult times is genuine gratitude for the blessings we have. That's the secret of being knocked down and getting back up. That's my definition of resiliency! Be grateful for what God has given you and blessed you with.

In closing, **I would like to invite you to a webpage, www.MikeGarciaFireChief.com/jumpstart, where I've written out the complete account of that night in Aurora, Colorado on July 20, 2012, along with recognition of the 13 who lost their lives that day.** They will never be forgotten as long as they are remembered by us. In addition, you can watch some added videos and get more information about me and how our Peer Support Group can help your community or organization.

ABOUT THE AUTHOR
R. MIKE GARCIA

Ray Michael Garcia "Mike" is a retired professional firefighter with 38 years of dedicated service, including 9 years as Aurora Colorado Fire Chief. He strongly believes in servant leadership and life-long learning. Mike has a Bachelor of Arts degree from the University of Colorado in Political Science, emphasis in Public Administration. He is a graduate of the prestigious National Fire Academy's Executive Fire Officer Program. Throughout his career he has held elite leadership assignments, including Training Chief. He's is the recipient of the Humanitarian of the Year. His passion now is sharing his experience and knowledge through Consulting, Training and Speaking.

Jumpstart Your Website

12 Crucial Must-Haves for Your Website

By Katrina Sawa

What do you need to know about websites when you're a business owner? It can be really overwhelming, I get it.

There are a lot of do-it-yourself templates out there where you can just design your site yourself and the templates make it easy (supposedly).

There are a lot of website designers and developers out there too, many with a whole host of different options to choose from at all different price points.

How do you choose WHAT you need or WHO to go to for help?

Well, this is one of the biggest things people want to discuss (or need to discuss) on their initial call with me.

As a business coach since 2002, I've helped thousands of entrepreneurs build their businesses, and my coaching has included helping them learn more about what to do with their websites.

How are you positioning yourself?

How are you presenting yourself?

I see a lot of entrepreneurs who are:

- trying to create their own website
- trying to create their own marketing materials
- struggling to create packages and pricing by themselves

It's critical that you do certain things to set yourself up as an expert. And this is what I mean by "positioning yourself."

Positioning can mean a few different things, such as:

- Are you confident? Do you give the impression that you know your "shit"?
- What YOU personally look and dress like in public (most of the time)
- What you look like online – websites, social media – your online graphics and branding

- How you price your products, programs and services: are you too cheap, too high, just right, have a good range?

- Do you give too much access to yourself without charging for your time?

- How personal you get – videos on your site or live videos on social media

- How you "show up" at events – as a speaker, exhibitor, attendee

- How you "show up" online – on virtual calls and networking: do you show up without makeup and hair done, wearing sweats, tennis shoes, or dressed like you would when you're going to a live event?

- Are you "connected?" Do you align yourself with the right people, celebrities, or industry leaders?

After you figure out how you want to position yourself overall, you can then start thinking about how you want your website to look.

The "look and feel" is the first thing you want to think about in regards to your website. Have a look at other people's websites in your industry (or even in other industries) to get outside-the-box ideas and see what you like and don't like. Be careful though, because you may like a website or two that are not technically or functionally good, so always heed the advice of someone like me in addition to other website designers, to make sure you're looking at websites that are going to "work" for you and your type of business.

Then, it's time to find the right web designer (which, unfortunately, isn't easy to do the first time around).

When you're interviewing website designers (yes, *you should interview* at least 2-4 people!), you need to make sure they agree with and/or are aware of the following 12 Crucial Must-Haves for your website. Otherwise, keep looking.

12 Crucial Must-Haves for Your Website.

Your website should be designed so that it can:

1. Be easily found on the search engines organically – this means you need a lot of keyword-rich content.

2. Increase visitor conversions - this means you must have ways for visitors to act on your website, otherwise they may leave and never come back. You can create free gifts, audios, reports, videos and more, then offer them a chance to get it if they give you their email address. That's one way.

3. Be updated regularly with new exciting, keyword-rich content and keep up to date with your technical website updates: without doing the basic updates, you could get hacked.

4. Have a professional, eye-catching "look and feel" for your branding and positioning (NOT done by YOU!).

5. Be built with the user in mind – this means making it easy for visitors to find things, sign up for things, buy things, and navigate easily without frustration or long load times.

6. Be extremely attention-grabbing on every page, especially the home page. This doesn't mean you have to be super-flashy, but don't be so subtle that nothing stands out. You can use pops of color, bigger fonts, bolder subheadlines, emotion-engaging images, and more.

7. Have a way for visitors to sign up on your list in order to build your database – this should be your number one goal with your website! This way, you can continue marketing to them. Otherwise, if they leave your site and aren't interested in anything right when they get there, they may never return.

8. Provide free resources to keep visitors coming back, including links, PDFs, other resources, and even blog posts and content.

9. Continue to build your relationship with your visitors, clients, and prospects using videos of you. Try to be personal and detailed with your content.

10. Have an easy way to contact you – it shocks me how often this is overlooked. Put your full contact information on your website. It's against the law, if you plan to sell anything from your website, NOT to list your mailing address or physical address (and yes, it can be a PO Box). Plus, it's frustrating as a visitor to not be able to find the email address or phone number of the website owner when you want it.

11. Tell your story and explain why you're doing what you're doing.

12. Perhaps add fun, interactive ways to get to know you or find out more, such as with videos, tutorials, frequently asked questions, quizzes, assessments, and online forms. The technology these days makes it very easy to do a lot of these things automatically (which is what you want!).

Your website must be designed strategically to do many other things as well; it should be the "hub" of your business. Plan to make updates or design a new website every couple of years, as technology changes quite a bit; you need to stay up to date.

If you're in the market for a new website now, or if you know it's time to update your current site, I'd urge you to talk to me first in a complementary business and website strategy session. Plus, I can refer you to the right website designer for you, and we can help you outline what you need and want. Sign up online for a call with me at www.AskKat.biz.

If you're ready to dive in now, then you can sign up for a JumpStart Your Website Consult and Planning Meeting. You can read all about it at www.JumpStartYourWebsite.net We go into depth in this series of calls, and I also work out a written plan for you to hand to your designer (or I'll refer you to one of mine) which will make it so easy for them to create a really effective, results-oriented site for you.

We can also review and audit your current site, talk about marketing of it, and I'll tell you everything I think you should change, add, or delete in order to get better results. Whether you use me and my team or not, don't wait too much longer to better position yourself online!

ABOUT THE AUTHOR
KATRINA SAWA

Katrina Sawa is an award-winning international speaker and business coach known as the JumpStart Your Biz Coach, because she kicks her clients and their businesses into high gear! She is the creator of The JumpStart Your Marketing® System, Jumpstart Your Business in 90 Days System, author of *Love Yourself Successful,* and International best-selling author of *Jumpstart Your New Business Now,* and 4 other books, 10 total to date. She loves to inspire and educate other entrepreneurs on how create a strategy to develop, market, and monetize a consistent money-making business doing what they love.

What's Next?

What did you think of the stories and expertise that our authors had to share?

Did you learn a few new things to take back to your life or work?

My hope is that you did learn a few things, or at least walk away with a fresh new way of thinking about some of our topics. If so, please go over to Amazon and leave us a review!

Our authors have been hand-selected due to their level of expertise, genuine integrity, and overall skill level in their industry. If you enjoyed reading some of their stories or learning more about how they help their clients, please take the next step and reach out to those who spoke to you.

Most of the authors in this book speak to groups of all sizes, both in person and virtually. They also offer products, programs, events, and services that can support you in one or more areas of your life, health, or business / career.

I highly recommend that you take advantage of their special offers, additional downloads, and more when you visit each of the websites listed within their chapters.

In addition, I've put together ONE page on my website where you can access all of their websites and special offers, to make it easy for you to follow up. **Go to www.JumpstartBookAuthors.com** right now, before you forget who you wanted to connect with or find out more about.

Thank you for reading this book, and I look forward to bringing you more Jumpstart Your _____ Authors in upcoming books, plus more training and teachings in my own books.

If you are an author who has something that YOU help people JUMPSTART and you would like to be considered as one of our next Jumpstart Authors, please go to www.JumpstartYourMarketing.com/JumpstartCompilation now and apply!

What Do You Help Your Clients Jumpstart?

In the Jumpstart Your _____ book series, YOU Fill in the Blank with the thing YOU do with YOUR clients for YOUR chapter, and become an author this year! Use this book as a MARKETING TOOL to get leads and grow your business.

Interested in becoming an author easily?

Get into a compilation book of 20-30 authors and write ONE chapter, but get huge exposure for you and your business, along with every author promoting it alongside you! Attract new clients and make more money after your prospects are introduced to you in this book.

Want to get more exposure, speaking gigs, or clients in the coming year? Become an author!

While it could take a while for you to write your own full book, it's relatively easy to get published in an anthology book by just writing one chapter. Everyone in the book promotes the books and sells them, so you get in front of a lot more people than you would with just your own book. PLUS... I do all the work! **Find out how this could benefit you here:**

www.JumpstartYourMarketing.com/ JumpstartCompilation

ABOUT KATRINA SAWA
COMPILATION PUBLISHER WITH JUMPSTART PUBLISHING

Katrina Sawa is known as the JumpStart Your Biz Coach because she kicks her clients and their businesses into high gear, both online and offline.

Katrina is the creator of the JumpStart Your Marketing® System, JumpStart Your Business in 90 Days System, and Jumpstart Yourself as a Speaker System. She is the author of nine other books including: *Love Yourself Successful, Jumpstart Your New Business Now, Jumpstart Your ____, Vol I, Power and Soul* with Ali Brown, *Entrepreneur Success Stories* with Loral Langemeier, *40/40 Rules* with a variety of women over 40, *The Itty Bitty Book of Words, My Journey My Journal,* and *Success Rituals 2.0* with a variety of other online marketers. *Jumpstart Your _____, Vol II* is Katrina's second hosted anthology book.

Katrina helps entrepreneurs make smarter marketing and business decisions in order to create the life and business of their dreams. She helps them create a big-picture vision, plan, and initial offerings, if they are just starting out.

Kat helps more seasoned entrepreneurs develop a more leveraged, efficient business and marketing plan. Either way, she shows clients all the steps, systems, and marketing that need to be put in place in order to accomplish their big-picture business, life, and money goals.

One thing that makes Katrina different is that she also focuses on her clients' personal lives. She found that most business owners lack enough self-confidence to truly enable them to get to their next level, or take those leaps of faith they need to achieve their ultimate dreams. Katrina's goal is to inspire, motivate, and educate entrepreneurs on how to love themselves fully, live a bigger life, and leverage themselves to complete happiness.

Katrina has a degree in Business Administration, Marketing Concentration, from California State University Sacramento, and has been a featured business expert on three of her local television news channels throughout her career thus far.

Katrina lives in Northern California with her husband Jason, step-daughter Riley, and their two rescued German Shepherds, Willow and Jake. She gives back to her community, speaks all over the world (in person and virtually), and she is very accessible to her clients with many options for getting the support they need.

You can find out all about Kat and her products, programs, services, and live events online at www.JumpstartYourMarketing.com.

Motivate and Inspire Others!

"Share this Book"

Retail $16.95 + Tax & Shipping

Special Quantity Discounts

5 - 15 Books	$11.95 Each
16 - 30 Books	$9.95 Each
30 - 1,000 Books	$7.95 Each

To Place an Order Contact:

K. Sawa Marketing International Inc.
916-872-4000
info@JumpstartYourMarketing.com
or go to
www.JumpstartYourMarketing.com/orderbooks

Grab One or More of the Jumpstart Your Business Free Trainings Now!

Learn How to:

- Get Started Speaking
- Jumpstart Your Business
- Implement Best Marketing Practices
- Build an Effective Website
- Create a Life You Love
- Find Your Purpose
- Love Yourself Successful
- Delegate & Build Your Team
- And more!

Get Access Online at:
www.JumpstartYourMarketing.com/FreeTrainings

Want a Deeper Training on How to Start, Grow, Market & Monetize Your Business?

- In Depth Training, How-To, Templates
- Roadmap & Plan to Jumpstart Your Biz
- Hot Seat Coaching
- Learn from Topic Specific Speakers
- Mastermind & Network
- Make Money with Easy YES Offers

Attend One of Kat's Live Events! Get Information at www.LiveBigEvents.com

Special BONUS Gift For You

To help you Jumpstart Your Business Now there are **FREE BONUS RESOURCES** for you at:

 **www.JumpstartGift.com**

Get your **3 FREE** in-depth training videos sharing how entrepreneurs can build a consistently profitable business doing what you love! PLUS, **FREE** ticket to a Live Big Event!

www.JumpstartGift.com

To Contact or Book Katrina to Speak:

K. Sawa Marketing International Inc.

PO Box 6
Roseville, CA 95661
916-872-4000
info@KatrinaSawa.com
www.KatrinaSawa.com
www.JumpstartYourMarketing.com